BATTLESHIP

EIGHT SHIPS THAT SHAPE YOUR SHIP-SHIPSHAPE!

A SPECIAL THANKS TO:
Robert Byers for words that work, as well as the RUI editorial team led by Joy Kingsbury and assisted by Wendy Burks.

Cover Design: Benjamin Smith and Jeremy N. Jones
Interior Layout: Jeremy N. Jones

REFORMERS UNANIMOUS INTERNATIONAL

PO Box 15732, Rockford, IL 61132
Visit our website at www.reformu.com.
Printed in Canada

Curington, Steven B., 1965-
Battleship: Eight Ships That Shape Your Ship—Shipshape!
Steven Curington.

ISBN 978-1-60725-103-3

BATTLESHIP

—EIGHT SHIPS THAT SHAPE YOUR SHIP—SHIPSHAPE!—

STEVEN B. CURINGTON

DEDICATION

This book is dedicated to two individual groups that form one army—our battle fleet. It is dedicated first of all to *teachers* (ship builders). Your dedication to building your students is to be commended, appreciated, and heavenly rewarded. But it is also dedicated to *students* (battleships), whose love for the Lord has led them to extreme measures of commitment and development for their eventual deployment. May all of our teachers remain good students and may all of our students strive to become great teachers. My prayer is that we safely set sail and secure others along the way.

TABLE OF CONTENTS

INTRODUCTION

At the beginning of World War II, the *HMS Hood* was the pride of the British navy. Launched just before the end of World War I, the *Hood* was the first real battleship of the modern era, and the largest warship in the world. The standard battle cruiser design used on previous ships was updated with 5000 tons of extra armor. The *Hood's* massive fifteen-inch guns fired shells that each weighed over 1900 pounds.

In May of 1941, England received word that the German battleship *Bismarck* had set sail for the Atlantic Ocean. To prevent this threat to England's vital shipping lanes, the *Hood* was dispatched to hunt down and destroy the *Bismarck*. On the morning of May 24, the *Hood* found and engaged the *Bismarck*. But the added armor the *Hood* had received was mostly concentrated on her sides, leaving the deck **exposed to shells dropping at a sharp angle.** Just eleven minutes after the battle began, the *Hood* was hit by shells from the *Bismarck*, burst into flames, broke in half, and sank.

Of the more than 1400 men serving on board, **only three** were rescued alive! How sad! Fourteen hundred people counted on that ship for safety in battle. The exact cause of the *Hood's* destruction was not completely settled. The most common theory, and the one accepted by the board of inquiry that investigated the disaster, was that one or more of the shells fired from the *Bismarck* had penetrated what the enemy had predetermined would be the weakest part of the ship—the deck. The aimed shell hit the magazine where *Hood's* ammunition was stored. Thus, this great ship, was destroyed from within, by the very ammunitions her maker had designed to protect her and save the lives of others. Whatever the cause, the *Hood's* destruction was a great blow to Britain's pride and confidence. The ship was simply not prepared and properly equipped for the battle.

Every one of us is involved in a great spiritual battle. The Christian life is not a luxury cruise; it is all out war. You are a battleship, whether you want to be or not. But that brings up a question: Are you competent to design and build not only your own battleship, but the battleship of those who God had led you to develop for battle? Do you know how to prepare your life for the attacks of the enemy? How is your armor? Are you loaded down in some parts and obviously exposed in others? Are you confident that you can survive a direct hit to the weakest part of your battleship? Do you know how to shore up your ship for battle? These things we must learn to discern before we set sail. Stay docked if you will, but remember Pearl Harbor? Some of those ships sank as well. Sitting ships are even more easily sunken ships!

In Battleship: Eight Ships that Shape Your Ship— Shipshape!, we will seek to show you what we at Reformers Unanimous International Ministries feel are the most important *ships* for shaping a battleship. We will use portions of our program to explain each, and where appropriate, use excerpts from our books to expose you to our total program commitment to this shipbuilding process. We hope that we can help you as a new believer, or as a more tenured believer in the Lord, "stay afloat in your boat."

WORSHIP
COMMUNICATION WITH GOD

"God is a spirit, and they that worship him must worship him in spirit and in truth." – **John 4:24**

The first ship that must be shaped properly in a new believer's life is their worship. Without a proper understanding of worship, we will surely sink into sin. Worship is the core purpose of God for every one of our lives. All of creation is intended by Him to be centered on His glory and praise. Psalm 19:1 says, "The heavens declare the glory of God."

The definition of the word *worship* comes from the meaning of the old English word *worthship*. The word *worthship* meant "a condition of being worthy of honor and respect."

Often, the word worship is misunderstood.

We tend to think that worship is going to church, singing songs, giving a percentage of our earnings to the church, and learning more of God through the teaching and preaching of the Bible. We DO worship when we do those things. But, doing them does not mean we are worshiping the way God wants, or as often as God wants. If we ought always to worship Him (Eph. 5:20), we understand that we cannot "always" be at church or even watching or hearing good preaching in other convenient ways. Thus, there must be more to worship than what many think.

As well, many believers know that worship is MORE than going to church, and they know it includes other "forms" of communication with God being done with frequency. However, that knowledge does not guarantee we will worship God more often as a result.

As a developing believer, it is imperative in your battle against the world, your flesh, and the devil that you understand your obligations to worship and exactly how to properly fulfill that obligation. Once these truths are lived, and you begin to exercise worship, you will soon experience the absolute privilege and joy of a life of worship.

WORSHIP IS COMMUNICATING COMMENDATION TO GOD.

Worship is best enjoyed and understood when we define it as "two-way communication with God." Worship is a daily pleasure, privilege, and yes, it is even a command. Ephesians 1:12 says, "That we should be to the praise of his glory." In private worship, we acknowledge in a particularly determined communicative style to God our appreciation for His incredible power, majesty, holiness, and glory. Without this private worship, we are not fulfilling God's plan and purpose... and we are not "ship-shape."

Public worship has similarities and differences to private worship. It is an assembly of believers who communicate their commendations to God in corporate praise, song, and sacrificial giving, very similar to their private or personal worship. However, public worship also consists of education through information *about* God. It is the preaching and teaching of the Word of God, that they might better understand Who He is and how they are to interact with Him in dedication and personal relation.

A few sentences ago, I indicated that God would have us worship Him in a "particularly determined communicative style." My friend, understanding the "what-is and the how-to" of this "particularly determined communicative style" is the key to enjoying our obligation to worship. More important than enjoying our *worship* is the *benefit* that comes from our worship when we use God's preordained, particularly determined style of communication.

What is this communication style that God commands from those who worship Him? John 4:24 gives us the acceptable communication style of our worship—"God is a Spirit: and they that worship him must worship him in spirit and in truth." God is a Spirit. So, if He is a Spirit, how then are we supposed to communicate with Him? Our answer is in the next phrase of our verse—"they that worship him must worship him in spirit and in truth."

So, here is God's "particularly determined style

of communication." We MUST worship Him in one way and only one way: "spirit and in truth." Though we will explain what that means in a moment, please understand that if we are not worshiping Him in this way, then we are not building a battle-ready battleship. In times of peace, when the enemy attack is absent, we will rest in calm waters and feel all is well. But, as soon as the enemy attacks with the shells of suggested sins, we will find ourselves vulnerable to "shell shock." We fall prey to struggles, for we have not engaged in proper preparation for our battle. Though we might not lose the battle, the war rages on! Why? It is because we have taken a direct hit to our ship. If we do not make corrections and better shape our battleship, eventually those mortars will affect our morals, and we will be sunk.

As a developing believer, if you are not following the "must" of John 4:24, then your vulnerability will eventually make you a casualty. If you are a teacher of developing believers, and you are not following, much less teaching this "must," you are doomed, and so are your students. Teachers, your ships will not last long in battle if you yourself do not know how to build one! We MUST worship Him in HIS predetermined communicative style.

The word *must* means "to be obligated." We are obligated to worship Him in spirit and in truth. I guess if we do not meet that obligation, then we are not worshiping Him the way that He wants. Would that not mean we are not worshiping? Or, would that mean we are worshiping, but not worshiping *Him*? If that is the case, then who are we worshiping? I think the answer is that we ARE worshiping Him, just not doing so correctly, and thus we worship improperly and ineffectively.

The verse prior to our key verse says, "But the hour cometh, and now is, when the true worshippers shall worship the Father in spirit and in truth: for the Father seeketh such to worship him" (John 4:23). Jesus proclaimed that in this new dispensation, there will be a two-way personal communication in spirit and in truth with God. He termed those who participated in this worship as *true worshipers*. I do not believe the Lord is saying that those who fail to worship in spirit and in truth are false worshipers. Rather, they are simply worshiping falsely. The word *falsely* means "in a manner contrary to truth."

That begs the question, "What is the truth?" The answer is this: It is not a *what*, it is a *Who*. It is He, Christ Jesus. He is the Truth (John 14:6). So, when we worship privately or publicly in corporate worship in a manner contrary to Jesus (Truth), it is unlikely to be appreciated, for God does not appreciate what He does not initiate!

John 4:23 goes on to say, "The Father seeketh such to worship him." Our heavenly Father is in search for those who will enunciate to him "communication of commendation" in spirit and in truth. Without it, it isn't the type of worship that meets our obligation as His creation, neither is it the form of worship that will bring us pleasure and protection in life as we navigate the dark waters of battle.

In Mark 7:6, we receive from Jesus a very stark warning about fake or false worship. It reads, "[Jesus] answered and said unto them, Well hath Isaiah prophesied of you hypocrites, as it is written, This people honoreth me with lips, but their heart is far from me."

The word *hypocrite* is an Old English word for the modern English word "actor." These people who honor God with their speech, while their meditations are on something far different are only actors. But, notice the next statement found in verse 7— "Howbeit in vain do they worship me." Our offerings of praise to God in worship are lies, vanities, and useless if they are not emanating from the heart both during and between our times of private and public worship.

So, what does it mean to worship Him in spirit and in truth? It simply means that because God is a Spirit, we must worship God through that portion of our trichotomy (body, soul, and spirit.) After our conversion, it is in our spirit, that the Holy Spirit comes to dwell. His Spirit and my spirit dwell together and are to live in unity. The Bible calls this part of me my inner man. It is within my inner man that God's clear communication is delivered to me. This communication comes, however, through a portal, if you will. That portal is the "Truth;" it is Jesus. God communicates to me in my spirit through Jesus the Truth. So, when the

Bible tells us we MUST worship God in spirit and in truth, it means our communication will be *in*, or surrounded by the limits of, the spirit and the truth.

Communication in spirit and in truth is our privilege that results from our Savior's sacrifice on Calvary. The veil was rent in two that we might have access to God. His communication stream is as follows:

1. It is spiritual. It is not physical or human in nature. It is not natural, it is supernatural.
2. It is communicated by God through Jesus Christ to His Spirit.
3. It is communicated TO my spirit by His Spirit.

Likewise, it is my spirit that communicates to His Spirit my thoughts for Him, by way of Jesus Christ. We see this truth clearly taught to the disciples by Jesus in John 16:13-15, where we read, "Howbeit when he, the Spirit of truth, is come, he will **guide you** into all truth: for he shall not speak of himself; **but whatsoever he shall hear, that shall he speak:**

and **he will show you things to come.** He shall **glorify me**: for he shall **receive of mine**, and shall **show it unto you**. All things that the Father hath are mine: therefore said I, that he shall take of mine, and shall show unto you."

I have listed below what Jesus said would be the role of the indwelling Holy Spirit:

1. He will guide you. (instruction and direction)

2. He will speak whatever He hears. (enunciation and communication)

3. He will hear from Jesus. (interpretation and interaction)

4. He will show us things to come. (illumination and revelation)

One may say he cannot hear from God. That is evidence of a spiritual problem. The problem is not so much that they do not know how to hear from God; it is that they do not believe. It is this Spirit that communicates our needs to God. This is God's way of communication. Romans 8:26 tells us that, "the Spirit itself maketh intercession for us with groanings which cannot be uttered."

The Spirit intercedes for us. *Intercede* is an Old English word for the modern English word "mediate." The Spirit does not mediate between us and God. Jesus mediates between us and God (I Tim. 2:5). Jesus is *our* Intercessor. But rather, the Spirit, Whom we see is the Spirit of Truth (the Spirit of Jesus) intercedes on behalf of Jesus with us! He mediates between Jesus and us. He does this "for us." That means for our benefit. Why? Because we "know not" what we need. But He does!

When we are not doing as we should, or we do not understand the errors of our way, He is there between us and Christ to mediate that we might make right our wrongs. He does this through "groanings which cannot be uttered."

The phrase "groanings which cannot be uttered" is not talking about moaning in some prayer language as some falsely teach. The word *groaning* is a "low, mournful sound." The word *uttered* means "to speak." Thus, we learn that the Holy Spirit communicates what God has given to Jesus on our behalf. He does this to us in a low, mourning sound that cannot be spoken. Thus, we do NOT hear words, but rather we are given persuasive promptings from our Spirit. Through this unique form of persuasion, the Spirit will place burdens on our heart that we might consider a change or seek answers for change from God. Once our heart (which is our meditator) is turned toward the "voice of the Shepherd," then God can clearly guide us through the Spirit of Christ Jesus.

Paul also taught this form of Spiritual communiqué as being the will of God in Romans 8:27—"he that searcheth the hearts knoweth what the mind of the Spirit, because he maketh intercession for the saints according to God." My friend, this is the way God wants it to be.

If we will allow the Spirit through the burden of persuasive groanings to "mediate that on which we meditate," we will find ourselves hearing from God and in turn He will hear from us as He has designed—in spirit and in truth.

So, we see that true worship takes place in the spirit. Worship is not a function of the mind, the will, or the emotions. Much of what we see in our "talks with God" today is nothing more that creative thinking. Often times, we, as soul-driven believers, rely too much on our own thought processes. God does not communicate to our mind, our will, or our emotions. He communicates to our spirit (through His Spirit, by Jesus). It is my spirit that communicates to my mind, it is my mind that negotiates with my will, and it is my will that motivates my emotions. Once all three are in line with my spirit's leading, then my body will carry forth God's will. In this condition, I am effectively walking in the Spirit. This will keep me from doing what I think, want, or feel in my mind, will, or emotions (that is, from fulfilling the lusts of my flesh).

If you look around at our world today, you see many things being called worship that are focused on outward expressions and are emotionally driven. Yes, there is a time and a place for public and corporate worship of God. But outward, corporate worship must begin inwardly. It must emanate from my inner man and travel through God's communication portals of His Son and Spirit in order to get to Him.

The story of Elijah on Mount Carmel illustrates this truth for us. The prophets of Baal leaped and shouted and even cut themselves as they prayed for fire to burn up their sacrifice. What did Elijah do? He quietly and calmly prayed. True worship is inner worship, taking place in the spirit.

It is impossible to separate Jesus Christ from our worship with God. Jesus taught us, "I am the way, the truth, and the life: no man cometh unto the Father, but by me" (John 14:6). The book of Revelation tells us that in Heaven, there is no temple; no building for worship. Why? "And I saw no temple therein: for the Lord God Almighty and the Lamb are the temple of it" (Rev. 21:22).

When we worship God, offering our thanks to Him for what He has done for us and expressing our praise to Him for Who He is pleases God. "I will praise the name of the God with a song, and will magnify him with thanksgiving. This also shall please the Lord..." (Psalm 69:30-31). The dictionary defines *praise* as "to give credit." There are three options when it comes to credit. We can give credit, take credit, or withhold credit.

When it comes to God, only one of those options is acceptable worship. Every good thing that we have in our lives comes to us from Him (James 1:17). It is not our wisdom or power or intelligence that brings us success; it is the mercy and grace of God. Therefore, only He deserves the worship and credit. Revelation 5:12 says, "Worthy is the Lamb that was slain to receive power, and riches, and wisdom, and strength, and honour, and glory, and blessing."

When we reject God's predetermined communicative pattern and choose rather to talk to God on our own terms, we waste our time, not His; for our sins have separated us from Him, and thus, He cannot hear us (Is. 59:2). This is our pride and God does not carry on in communication with people who are proud.

Pride destroys worship because pride encourages us to withhold credit from God or take the credit for ourselves. God will not share His glory with anyone (Is. 42:8). Our sincere attempt to reflect the glory and honor to God is an expression of our worship—our declaration that He is worthy. Our reaction to compliments and the praise of others reveals whether or not we have been worshiping God in our spirit. Do we take it for ourselves, or do we give it to Him? There are certainly many things for which we can express our gratitude and praise to God.

Praise God for His love and kindness to us.
Psalm 63:3 – "Because thy lovingkindness is better than life, my lips shall praise thee."

Praise God collectively—as part of a church, Sunday School class, or RU meeting.
Psalm 67:3 – "Let the people praise thee, O God; let all the people praise thee."

Praise God throughout the day.
Psalm 71:8 – "Let my mouth be filled with thy praise and with thy honour all the day."

Praise God for the span of our life.
Psalm 71:14-15 – "But I will hope continually, and will yet praise thee more and more. My mouth shall shew forth thy righteousness and thy salvation all the day; for I know not the numbers thereof."

Praise God for salvation.
Psalm 71:23 – "My lips shall greatly rejoice when I sing unto thee; and my soul, which thou hast redeemed."

Praise God for His goodness and works done on our behalf.
Psalm 107:31 – "Oh that men would praise the LORD for his goodness, and for his wonderful works to the children of men!"

Praise God throughout the day for His right decisions on our behalf.
Psalm 119:164 – "Seven times a day do I praise thee because of thy righteous judgments."

Praise God in front of your children for His efforts and actions on our (and their) behalf.
Psalm 145:4,10 – "One generation shall praise thy works to another, and shall declare thy mighty acts. All thy works shall praise thee, O LORD; and thy saints shall bless thee.

Praise God for what He is going to do on our behalf, in advance!
Psalm 42:5 – "Why art thou cast down, O my soul?

and why art thou disquieted in me? hope thou in God: for I shall yet praise him for the help of his countenance."

In the model prayer, Jesus established a pattern for us beginning our prayer time with praise to the Father. "And he said unto them, When ye pray, say, Our Father which art in heaven, Hallowed be thy name. Thy kingdom come. Thy will be done, as in heaven, so in earth" (Luke 11:2). Why should we start our prayer with praise? It is because praise prepares our hearts, acknowledging that God is the source of every good gift.

Praising God pleases Him. Since we owe God the credit for every victory and for the lessons learned in every defeat, we ought to praise Him on both good days and on bad days. The Reformers Unanimous International "It's Personal" Daily Journal is a phenomenal tool used all across the world to track our worship. In it, it has set aside a time each day specifically for you to praise the Lord.

Praise is not automatic. It takes a conscious effort to praise the Lord throughout our day. And that effort begins by praising Him and giving Him the credit He is due in the morning and continuing it throughout the day.

If our worship has been "ship-shape," our view of God will be such that we know only He deserves to receive credit. We will thus worship Him and give Him **all** of the glory.

Developing Christians (which is really the entire body of Christ) must worship Him properly. Teachers, teach worship properly. If we do not, we shall sink from sin.- To build a better battleship, we need to learn and yearn to properly worship Him.

DISCIPLESHIP
HOW WE LEARN *ABOUT* GOD

"Come unto me, all ye that labour and are heavy laden, and I will give you rest. Take my yoke upon you, and learn of me; for I am meek and lowly in heart: and ye shall find rest unto your souls. For my yoke is easy, and my burden is light."
– Matthew 11:28-30

Every believer is called to be a disciple of Jesus Christ and to make disciples for Christ. The word *disciple* comes to us from the Latin word for learner. When He began His ministry, Jesus called twelve men to follow Him. For more than three years, they spent almost every waking moment with the Lord, watching Him work, listening to Him teach, observing Him pray and asking Him questions. Those first disciples were learning everything they could from Jesus.

Discipleship is getting to know *about* God from those who know Him. It is gaining valuable information about Him from those who have an intimate, personal relationship with Him. We need to know and learn everything about God that we can. Just as the first disciples learned from Jesus what the Father was like (John 14:7-10), we learn from the Holy Spirit and the Word. That means we are going to have to spend regular, consistent, scheduled time studying and meditating on the Scriptures.

DISCIPLESHIP IS INFORMATION ABOUT GOD.

There's an old saying that knowledge is power. It's very true in life; but in the Christian life, it's not what you know, it's Who you know that grants you power. But to know Him and to make Him known, we must learn of Him. The more we learn about God from His Word and others who know Him better, the more prepared we will be to live victoriously by faith.

The pattern of discipleship found in the Bible is that of continually learning. It is not a one-time process; but an ongoing program of instruction. For example, after Saul of Tarsus met God on the road to Damascus, he spent three years in the desert, being taught by God (Gal. 1:15-18). But yet, he later wrote, "Not as though I had already attained, either were already perfect: but I follow after, if that I may apprehend that for which also I am apprehended of Christ Jesus. Brethren, I count not myself to have apprehended: but this one thing I do, Forgetting those things which are behind, and reaching forth unto those things which are before" (Phil. 3:12-13).

The writer, Paul, was well-seasoned in his Christian life by this time, but he had learned one primary thing: to forget that which is behind and to press forward. We must be ever learning lest we fail to "come unto the knowledge of the truth" (I Tim. 2:4).

Knowing about God is not enough; we must move forward to knowing God. But we cannot know God until we know about Him. The secret of the victorious Christian life is the foundation of a personal, intimate relationship with God. This foundation is laid by acquiring information about

God, learning how He operates and lives through you, for His glory.

To build this foundation, we must learn how God acts. When we know how God acts, we can see when God is acting out or man is acting up! There are three behavior patterns for mankind. We can choose how God acts (1). We can choose how man acts (2). Or we can choose how man acts when he is trying to act like God in his own power (3). How God acts is righteousness (1). How man acts is unrighteousness (2). But when man tries to act like God? That is self righteousness (3). A self righteous man may be doing right, but he is doing it himself! God is not glorified.

Discipleship is learning these three behavior patterns that you may "understand" what and Who is right. From there, it will be your personal relationship with God that will get you right and keep you right.

The best tool for learning about God, as a disciple, is the Bible. We need do the following things with the Bible:

1. We need to read it daily.
2. We need to study it, when prompted, while reading.
3. We need to memorize portions of it often, when prompted, while studying.
4. We need to meditate upon it day and night and, when prompted, while in turmoil
5. We need to hear it as it is preached often, even more than is biblically required.

This pattern of learning will ensure plenty of information about God and stimulate a quicker development of your personal relationship with Him. Other books can and should be added, but careful consideration should be given to whose books you read and how much faith you place in their teachings, for they are far short of being God's words. To get a better grasp of God, you will be best served by the Bible and good books about the Bible.

One such good book that we use at Reformers Unanimous Ministries is the *Gaining Remaining Fruit Discipleship* Series. This series of books actually gives you "homework!" Of course, if you are a student and He is our Master Teacher, then obviously, you may need to "take some work home with you." That is what is meant by a discipleship course. The word *course* means "an orderly way of proceeding." So if discipleship is learning, we can thus conclude that a healthy and helpful "discipleship course" will be an "orderly way of proceeding in our learning about God."

That's what our GRF series will do for you. In a very orderly fashion, it will teach you many great things about our God that you may spiritually learn and grow. This discipleship course is made of three books that contain ten different phases. Each of these phases are broken up into twenty-seven sections. These sections include over three hundred personal "challenges." How's that for an orderly way of proceeding?!

Each book will take on average about six months to complete. Within about two years, working slowly at their own pace, almost everyone completes the course. The students are rewarded throughout as they reach different stages of completion. It is quite captivating, very motivating and, as thousands have said, definitely rewarding.

Let me explain to you what we teach in the GRF Study Course. The topics are listed below and then explained:

- You will learn the plan of salvation in the Challenger workbook.

- You will learn the nine fruits of the Spirit in the Strongholds Study Course.

- You will learn eighteen of the fruits of righteousness in the Uphold and Behold Study Course.

- You will learn twenty-seven offsetting works of self righteous flesh in all three study courses.

The course is intended to help you understand how God acts, how man acts, and how man acts when He is trying to act like God (that is to say, man doing good in his own power).

For clarity, I want to help you understand how we at RUI take on the grand challenge and great commission of making disciples by using our Gaining Remaining Fruit Series.

THE STRONGHOLDS STUDY COURSE

The first workbook of our Gaining Remaining Fruit Study Course is the "Strongholds." The Strongholds Study Course (black in color) consists of four phases, called the Challenger, Transformer, Conformer, and Reformer. The Challenger is a study in God's gift of justification. The other three phases are a study of sanctification. This study is an explanation of the nine fruits of the Spirit and the offsetting works of the flesh.

The Challenger phase teaches God's plan for building the foundation of your life. First Corinthians 3:11 tells us that there is really no other foundation that any man can lay other than that which was already laid. The Foundation which was already laid is Jesus Christ. God desires that everyone in His creation have a personal relationship with His Son, Jesus Christ. It is our first step to **freedom** on earth. This step also qualifies us for eternal life, which is obviously far more important. We begin at this step.

In this Challenger phase, you will learn **God's design for freedom**. It is rather simple to understand and easy to apply when we do it with our whole heart. God's design for **freedom** begins in John 14:6, where Jesus said, "I am the way, the truth, and the life…" When Jesus stated that He is the Truth, He was explaining that others may claim to have supernatural truth, but only He is capable of exposing the real Truth that comes from God. With this (Jesus is Truth) in mind, please read Jesus' formula for **freedom** from strongholds:

"Then said Jesus to those Jews which **believed on him**, If ye **continue in my word**, then are ye **my disciples** (followers) ; And ye shall **know** the truth (Jesus), and the **truth** (Jesus) shall make you free" (John 8:31-32).

Below are the steps to freedom from strongholds, as listed in the verse above:

1. Believe on Jesus
2. Continue (remain) in His Word (the Bible).
3. Follow Christ with your life (Disciple).
4. Your knowledge of Jesus will increase.
5. Jesus (not you) will make you free.

The Challenger phase covers step one of this process in deep detail. Choosing to become a disciple (a learner) will be the most important decision you will ever make in the Christian life. If you choose to do so as a student of our GRF series, may I remind you to stay focused on why you are doing this. At first, to some of you, this may seem elementary, but as you progress through the curriculum, you will see why God has brought it to you.

Once you have completed you Challenger phase, you will proceed to the Transformer, Conformer, and Reformer phases. In these phases, you will learn the following:

- **Phase Two** (Transformer phase) is a study in the fruits of the Spirit: love, joy, and peace versus the offsetting self righteous works of the flesh self love, frustration, and worry.

- **Phase Three** (Conformer phase) is a study in the fruits of the Spirit: longsuffering, gentleness and goodness versus the offsetting self righteous works of the flesh quick-tempered, harshness, and meanness.

- **Phase Four** (Reformer phase) is a study in the fruits of the Spirit: faith, meekness and temperance versus the offsetting self righteous works of the flesh doubt, discord, and self-indulgence.

By learning to yield to these fruits in your life, you will gain God's power over your sin and your interpersonal conflicts in life. This is the Strongholds Study Course and it is followed by the Uphold Study Course.

THE UPHOLD STUDY COURSE

The UPHOLD Study Course (blue in color) consists of three more phases. It is a study in nine personally chosen fruits of righteousness and their offsetting fruits of self righteousness. You see, when the Spirit of God comes to live within our lives, we receive His nature. His nature produces fruit. This is the nine fruits of the Spirit listed above. And once we gain His character, we can overcome all of life's difficulties, IF our walk remains IN the Spirit. However, eventually we can become good at these behaviors and sometime are quite capable of responding somewhat like God in but under our own power. That becomes self righteous flesh.

Understanding these behaviors is good, but

realizing you now have living within you the ability to live righteously is even better! However, when your walk with God wavers, you will need to be able to depend on yourself to do right, even when you don't want to! This is not easy. It takes not only the fruit of the Spirit to do right when you are willing; it takes good Christian character to do right when you are less than willing.

For that reason, we mature our students by training them in other fruits in addition to the fruit of the Spirit. You see the fruit of the Spirit is righteousness. Righteousness then also produces a fruit – the fruit of righteousness. We teach about these fruits in the Uphold and Behold Study Courses.

As we educated thousands of converts through our Strongholds Study Course, we learned that a great many people are lacking the basic character that other student disciples may have been more fortunate to learn when they were younger.

Some of these who had not developed that character would wonder, "Does this mean I will have a more difficult time living for the Lord?" The answer is "NO! Not at all." But, there is only one way to quickly overcome poor character issues. That is to embrace a Spirit-filled life that manifests itself in complete submission to the leading of our Lord.

Weakness is the modern English word for the Old English word *infirmity*. And Solomon, a wise man though he had many character issues himself, taught us in Proverbs 18.14a, "The spirit of a man will sustain his infirmity. . ."

Though everyone has some weakness in character, the weakest among us can become the greatest in the Kingdom of God; for when we are at our weakest, He is at His strongest (II Cor.12:10). But, it is not God's wish that we remain weak men or women of character. Character is defined by Webster's Dictionary as "a peculiar habit impressed on a person to distinguish him from another."

In other words, character is nothing more than good habits! It is our bad habits that brought us to need RU in the first place. It is Christ Who saved us from our bad habits, and it is He Who wants to assist us in developing good habits. And good habits you will have!

But, eventually, those good character qualities

can make you "comfortable." And now, because you are doing the right thing, and more often than not, you are doing it the right way, you have a tendency to lose touch with your developing spirit. I know many Christians who have great character, but their walk with God is so weak they live a frustrated and self-serving life. Character coupled with a dormant spirit leads to apathy. This spirit of apathy must be avoided at all costs!

As a reminder, the fruit of the Spirit produces **righteousness**. That means the fruit (or outcome) of the Spirit of God produces nine righteous actions or reactions to every difficult situation and circumstance in life.

But just as the Spirit offers a fruit (of righteousness), His righteousness also offers a fruit. The Bible calls it this "fruits of righteousness." It is actually the outcome of righteous living. Do you know what that is? It's having good habits. It's good character.

In other words, when we begin to live the Spirit-filled life, we will become better people who are capable of doing many good things in our own power. While that is better than *doing* wrong, it is not better than *being* right! Good will is no substitute for God's will!

Philippians 1:9-11 explains this beautiful Spirit-filled lifestyle like this: "this I pray, **that your love may abound** yet more and more in knowledge and in all judgment. . ." This encouragement is challenging us to abound in love as we grow in the Lord. His love abounds in us as we gain a more intimate personal relationship with the Lord (knowledge) and personal discernment in our spirit (judgment).

If we have that personal relationship and Spirit-led discernment, He goes on to say that we "may approve things that are excellent; that ye may be sincere and without offense till the day of Christ." WOW! That's some mighty fine character—sincerity and consistency!

How do we accomplish such a great work? We need a great walk, that's how! The end result of this type of walk is where we find the topics for the Uphold and Behold discipleship courses, "Being **filled** with **the fruits of righteousness**, which are

by Jesus Christ, unto the glory and praise of God."

His walk will fill us with His Spirit. The fruit of the Spirit will fill us with the fruit of righteousness. The fruits of righteousness, which is godly Christian character, are "by Jesus Christ." He does the work of Christianity (our salvation), and He wants to be the One Who does the work of developing Christian character. In other words, He gives characters character! And it is all done for one important reason: "to the glory and praise of God!"

THE UPHOLD AND BEHOLD STUDY COURSE

In the Uphold and Behold Study Course (which is gold in color), we expose, over the course of six phases, eighteen (nine in each book) character qualities that we must gain and retain as good habits in our lives. Good habits must be a result of the submissive promptings of the Spirit in order to qualify as a "work of the Lord." These phases are taught as follows:

- **Phase Five** is a study in the fruits of righteous: appreciation, compassion and forgiveness versus the offsetting works of self righteousness: ingratitude, indifference and bitterness.

- **Phase Six** is a study in the fruits of righteous: dependability, purity, and humility versus the offsetting works of self righteousness: inconsistency, immorality, and pride.

- **Phase Seven** is a study in the fruits of righteous: loyalty, contentment, and serviceability versus the offsetting works of self righteousness: skepticism, covetousness, and unreliability.

- **Phase Eight** is a study in the fruits of righteous: enthusiasm, hospitality, and self control versus the offsetting works of self righteousness: apathy, animosity, and uncontrolled.

- **Phase Nine** is a study in the fruits of righteous: initiative, diligence, and obedience versus the offsetting works of self righteousness: slothfulness, negligence, ostentatious.

- **Phase Ten** is a study in the fruits of righteous: patience, discretion, and tolerance versus the offsetting works of self righteousness: aggravation, unruliness, and narrow-mindedness.

Each of these phases have over 100 personal "challenges" that our students are required to complete in order to graduate from the discipleship program. They will memorize many things, study their Bible diligently. journal daily during intimate devotional time, write essays, and read three complete books written for their benefit. It is a very intense, but very complete, discipleship course. We trust if you join our student body of disciples of our Lord Jesus, it will not only be relevant to where you need to go in your personal pilgrimage with the Lord, but that it will remain real to you throughout your walk with Him.

In conclusion, as you train in these 27 fruits that God wants to prompt every one of His children into performing under His influence, you will grow in your knowledge *about* God. That knowledge, we believe will be the catalyst for your very own intimate and personal relationship *with* God. Why? It is because information *about* God is the **fuel** that a personal relation *with* God will **burn**!

RELATIONSHIP
HOW WE *KNOW* GOD

"That I may know him, and the power of his resurrection, and the fellowship of his sufferings, being made conformable unto his death."
– Philippians 3:10

The pattern of our relationship with God was set in the Garden of Eden before the fall of man. Daily, God would visit and talk to Adam. We were created to have that kind of close fellowship with Him. Nothing in life can substitute for it in the Christian life. You can no more have a vibrant spiritual life absent of a relationship with God than you can have a vibrant physical life absent of oxygen.

Relationship is us getting to know God. Knowing someone is far different from simply knowing about them. I have a friend who knows just about everything he could ever learn about D.L. Moody.

But no matter how much he knows about Moody, he will never *know* D. L. Moody. Obviously, it is because Moody is dead and gone to glory.

However, Jesus is very much alive and He longs to be a very real and present Presence in your life. It is not a stretch to say that our "ship of relationship" is the most important part of our ship. Without intimacy in your relationship with Him, no other part of the ship works as He intended. You may still worship, but it will be ineffective and full of apathy. You may disciple, but you will only gain knowledge. It will puff you up and leave you boasting of a God you only know a lot about.

Yes, indeed, without a dynamic love relationship with Him, we will find the Christian life to be a series of ups and downs, periods of self induced victory punctuated with bouts of self indulged defeat. For if we don't walk in intimacy with the Spirit, we will eventually walk, once again, in the immaturity of the flesh.

RELATIONSHIP IS INTIMACY WITH GOD.

The Hid-N-Life™is a term at RU that we use to

define this intimacy in Christ. Simply put, when it comes to true Christian living, it is not about *information*; it is about a personal *relation*. That intimacy only comes as we experience God's work of sanctification in our lives.

Have you struggled to experience that dynamic personal relation? Well, thanks to the prince of this world and his delegators (powers and authorities), the information needed to develop that personal relation often remains hidden! Just like the devil hides justification from the unbeliever, he hides the benefits of sanctification from the believer.

The Hid-N-Life™is best described as exercising a measure of confidence (that's faith) in God's ability to do the work (that's grace) necessary in my life to conform me to the image of His Son (that's fruit) through a daily walk with Him. I will not *do* the work (that's performing); I will allow the work to be done *in* me (that's transforming). I must realize that God did not come to change my life (that's self righteousness). He came to exchange it (that's righteousness)!

As a result, I will die daily through confession

and repentance of all sin that is obvious to me or brought to my conscience by the Holy Spirit during my daily time with God and throughout the day. As I do this, I will experience a greater enlightenment in my worship. My enlivened worship will then provide me with the most coveted act of the Spirit, and that is His intuition. With Holy Spirit intuition, I will remain the clean vessel required to qualify for God's power on my walk and work.

At the core of the various RU ministries is the goal of exposing this Hid-N-Life™ all believers to enjoy. God intends for our relationship with Him to be a catalyst for proper actions and reactions in the adversities of life. In order to enjoy His life, we must be purged of our own. This is allowed by God, that we may be purified for His use. The Bible say in Job 23:10 that, "when he hath tried me, I shall come forth as gold." James Aughey, an American pastor from the last century, it this way: "God brings men into deep waters not to drown them, but to cleanse them."

It is sad, but true, but most Christians choose apathy over adversity. But apathy never accomplished anything for God. If you or those students you teach develop apathy in their Christian life, you can be sure intimacy with Him will be non-existent. No battleship can navigate the waters of this world in apathetic angst and expect to enjoy a long-lasting victory. Smooth sailing is only possible in the midst of "Savior stimulated" storms. Author Charles C. West may have put it best when he said, "We turn to God for help when our foundations are shaking only to learn that it is God who is shaking them."

God has a school of learning for all of His student disciples. It is Adversity University™. You cannot expect to live godly in Christ Jesus without suffering persecution (II Tim. 3:12). But when our relationship with the Lord is sweet and special to us, we can remain calm in the stormy sea, recognizing the ship will sail smoothly, for we have set our sale firmly through a deep abiding relation*ship*!

Dr. Paul Kingsbury, my Pastor at North Love Baptist Church in Rockford, Illinois, wrote an entire book on this subject. The book is called <u>Adversity University: The Fraternity for Eternity</u>. It explains in great detail how God uses adversity, not primarily as chastening, but rather as training. It is this training that should be so coveted. For it is this learning process that not only *gets* us right with Him, but *keeps* us right as well.

At Reformers Unanimous, we call this process of learning "conforming by transforming." When we reject our adversity and embrace a lifestyle of Christian apathy, we will not please God. We will seek to please others and ourselves instead. In an effort to please others rather than Him, we will find that we are unable to experience that transformation process that we so desperately need to enjoy our positions as "peculiar people." Rather than "conforming by transforming" we will find ourselves "conforming by performing."

Again, I say, your relationship with Jesus Christ is and ought to be the most important relationship you will ever have! Christ considers His relationship with us preeminently important. In fact, it is so important that He sends people to Hell for not having one! But there is much more to this personal relationship than just being the property of God. There is more to it than just being Heaven bound. There is an intimate and personal relationship in which you are not only *known* by God, but one in which you may *know* Him, as well. How is your personal relationship? How well do you know God?

In the chapter "Personal Is Important" found in the devotional tool, the *"It's Personal"* Daily Journal, I illustrate relationship development with God by how my wife Lori developed a relationship with me. In the spring of 1994, as a 28-year-old bachelor, I met a young lady named Lori. Lori and I began to date, and over the course of the next few months, she really got to KNOW me. She did this in five different, discernible ways.

<u>Lori wrote me notes</u>. These were often short, simple notes with questions that required responses. I would write her back with all my thoughts on any given subject—long notes with long responses. We would discuss the notes at later dates, only to find she had read them so well, she had my words memorized! (I had no idea she would use them against me later!) She used this

written form of communication to get to KNOW me. I was more concerned about the way her letters smelled than what they contained. Her knowledge of me continued to grow and so did her personal relationship with me.

Lori wanted to be wherever I was going to be. Whether I was at a ball game with the guys, at the park with friends, or at church or on a church activity, she wanted to be in my presence whenever possible. She used that time to study me and watch me. It helped her get to KNOW me better. Being with me, wherever I was and as often as possible, increased the pace at which she got to know me. As a result, her personal relationship with me grew quickly.

Lori talked to me on the phone. I remember how she would ask me questions. These questions were not simple "yes" or "no" questions, but questions that would take explanations, 10-15-20 minute explanations. She really wanted to get to know me by listening to my responses to her questions and comments. She would ask me what I thought about something, and then she would be quiet. She would not respond back, leaving an uncomfortable pause in the air. I would continue to speak, and she would continue to listen, with little or no response to my discussion. This form of listening really gave her valuable insights into my personality that she used to get to know me better. I was content to do the majority of the talking during these phone conversations. Little did I know how important it was to spend time "getting to know her" during those lengthy phone conversations.

Lori talked to people who knew me. She got the scoop on me. She would question my friends about me. When we had disagreements, she got advice from a friend of mine, or someone else who knew me better than she knew me. She probably learned more about me through other people who knew me than she did by being with me. I, on the other hand, did not learn about Lori through her friends. When Lori did something that I did not understand, I would try to figure it out myself. I did not take the time to quiz her friends or to talk to those who knew her better than I did.

Lori asked lots of questions. It seemed like

nearly every time we were together, she would ask me about my standards and convictions on certain issues. She focused on my every opinion so that she could get to KNOW me better.

When Lori and I got married on May 25, 1995, she knew me very well; but unfortunately, I barely knew her. Rather, I knew me… and I have been playing catch up ever since! Lots of Christians approach God the same way. We simply don't make the investment to *know* Him, much less to make Him known (Eph. 6:19). That results in a one-sided personal relationship rather than healthy two-way conversations.

The best tool our ministry will offer you as assistance for your development of a dynamic, love relationship with Jesus Christ is the book I mentioned, the *"It's Personal"* Daily Journal. This journal, which is our top-selling item, has been the very key and catalyst in my own personal relationship with Christ since it was first designed in 1999.

The *"It's Personal"* Daily Journal is a proven method for developing your own personal intimacy with Christ. It uses what I term "God's five forms of communication." These five forms mirror the forms of communication that my wife used (described above) to develop her relationship with me. I encourage everyone I counsel, whether newly born baby believers or decades old (but apathetic tenured) believers, to engage in the *"It's Personal"* Daily Journal. It is well used by thousands of satisfied customers.

Again, I reiterate. We MUST put our relationship with Christ as our first and foremost priority in life. He should receive our first fruit - an early morning quiet time engaged in daily devotions is a minimum to see that relationship grow and develop.

This chapter's key verse explains the formula, if you will, for developing a dynamic personal relationship with Christ. Paul said, "That I may know him and the power of his resurrection, and the fellowship of his suffering, being made conformable unto his death" (Phil. 3:10). Notice the progression: Paul wants to know Jesus, the resurrection, the suffering and finally, the crucifixion. Why did Paul place things in that order? Why end with the crucifixion? That wasn't the last event in the series of things that happened to Jesus; it was the first one. Paul is talking about a process of events in inverted order.

You cannot know Jesus without going through these steps in the right order. Many believers never get past the crucifixion. They have accepted the death of Jesus as the payment for their sins and trust Him as Savior, yet they never move further beyond being known by Him. They never get to know Him themselves. They never walk in familiarity with the suffering for the sake of others that He endured. They never rise up in power to a new life through the Holy Spirit as He did. They never truly know Him.

I describe it this way: these people never turn their crucifixion into a resurrection. I explain this process of death, burial and resurrection in our topical books for addiction recovery. However, in my book Today I Lay, I explain this truth in much deeper detail. I would like to refer to some of the information from that book:

Those who never turn their crucifixion into a

resurrection are believers who have died to the old life, but they have not received a new life to replace it. People who have things or people whose things have them cannot go through this process. You must count all things as loss (Phil. 3:8). That is the first step on the path to a personal relation with Jesus Christ.

Knowing Jesus requires an experience of the great power that only comes with resurrection. But you cannot be resurrected unless you first die. Also, you are not ready for the resurrection until you have spent those three days in the tomb, developing that intimate familiarity with Jesus. To have that, you must be conformed to His death.

Notice that Philippians 3:10 does not say, "being conformed to his death." But rather, the verse says, "being *made* conformable unto his death." This is not a process we want to do—it is something God *makes* us do. He will make us conform to the image of Christ's death, and we must allow Him to do so if we are to enjoy the intimate fellowship with Him that transforms our hearts. This is not a one time process… it must continue day after day. In fact,

Paul said, "I die daily" (Gal. 2:20).

We have to be willing to die in order to reach this level. What does Paul mean when he talks about being conformed—molded—to the death of Christ? What kind of form was His death? Crucifixion was one of the most brutal and harsh means of execution ever devised. It was a slow and painful death, often lasting for days if the prisoner was strong and in good physical condition.

It is also important to remember that Jesus did not die as a payment for His own sins. He was the holy, innocent, spotless Lamb of God. He died for others. It is not as difficult for us to reach the point where we are willing to face up to the consequences for our actions. (That does not mean it is easy, just that it is easier than suffering for others.) The form of the crucifixion was suffering, not just for the sins of others, but for the sake of others. That is the form to which we must be molded.

This is something God wants to make us do, yet many believers never go through the process. We are not willing to suffer because of the weaknesses or sins of others, or for the sake of others. As a result, we miss out on the glorious resurrection power and the intimate fellowship with Jesus that is the secret to victorious living.

Why do so many churches struggle to get their members involved in the ministry? Why do pastors have to plead for workers or for people to go out and share the gospel? Why are so many only interested in what they can receive, without being willing to give? Simply put, because they are not formed to the mold of Christ's death on the cross. They are willing to receive the benefits of salvation, but they are not willing to yield to God's direction to take up the cross and follow Jesus.

We will never experience intimate relationship with Him until we are willing to put up with inconveniences for the sake of others. When the pastor asks for someone to help with a ministry, and you feel an inward persuasion that you should help, who do you think that is? Is it the devil? Does he want you to be involved in reaching others? Well then, pray tell, by process of elimination, who is it? It is the Holy Spirit of God, moving you to live as Jesus died—for the sake of others.

So many times we hear the call from our authority (the pastor or another leader) and the persuasion of the Spirit, and do not respond because it means we would have to sacrifice. Yet that is the suffering that we must become part of in order to have an intimate knowledge of Christ.

Good things—the recliner, the football season, the 24-hour news channel, the hobby—can get in the way and keep you from knowing Jesus, if you are not willing to give them up to meet the needs of others. Again, this kind of sacrifice is not a natural response. It requires being conformed, or as Paul said, "being made conformable" and God is able to either make us or break us if we are not willing to yield to Him to become daily dying people.

We are not naturally given to be poured into the mold of sacrificing for others. One thing I learned very quickly when we started Reformers Unanimous is that people don't mess up between eight and five. (Well, maybe eight p.m. to five a.m.!) The problems that people have and the struggles they face don't fit the business day. When they sin, they call for help. Sometimes we have to get out of bed to go to the rescue. You won't do that unless you are willing to suffer for the sins of others. That's not natural! It's supernatural. It only happens as we yield to the internal persuasion of the Spirit.

As we enter into His fellowship, we will experience great pain periods of turmoil in life. When you make the commitment to reach out, sacrificing yourself for the needs and sake of others, the road is not going to be smooth. So many people are surprised when things go wrong. But Peter said, "Beloved, *think it not strange* concerning the fiery trial which is to try you, as though some thing happened unto you" (I Pet. 4:12). In other words, don't think something strange is happening when you are facing fiery trials. You should expect them; when you live IN Christ, trouble is coming!

The Apostle Paul experienced this is his own life. He had been greatly empowered to preach the gospel effectively. He had seen numerous churches established and many people saved. He had been given visions from God that no one else had. He also suffered greatly with what he termed "a thorn in the flesh" (II Cor. 12:7-10). He realized it came from Satan, and he eventually learned that God would not remove it from his life. He was forced to accept His weakness. But pay careful attention to what Paul eventually concluded in my paraphrase of this passage: "His grace is sufficient for me, for His strength is made perfect through my weaknesses." Paul stopped fighting his suffering. Instead he said "I take pleasure" in the things that hindered him! Paul was willing to trade his strength for God's strength through suffering to enjoy intimate fellowship with Him.

I believe a lot of us spend much of our time in prayer asking God to take away the painful things in our life that are His gifts to us! We expect our gain to be replaced with greater gain when we yield it to God. Instead, we find it replaced with pain. That's the "fellowship of his suffering."

Prior to His path leading to Calvary, Jesus earnestly prayed, asking His Father for the cup to pass from Him. Did the cup pass? Why not? Didn't the Father love the Son? Of course He did. But it was God's will—His purpose and His plan—that Jesus should suffer. What Jesus experienced was

God-ordained adversity.

I have some news for you today. God has some adversity planned for you. That adversity is not intended to drive you back into the world. Instead, it is meant to drive you deeper into your relationship with Jesus. It is meant to make you rely on Him more than ever before. Through that suffering, we experience intimate familiarity with Jesus.

If you pay attention to the definition of the words as you read the New Testament, you will find some things that don't seem to belong together. Next to words that describe great pain, suffering, distress and torture we find words of joy and peace. Let me show you some examples of what I mean.

Paul said, "And I will very **gladly** spend and be spent for you; though the **more abundantly I love you, the less I be loved**" (II Cor. 12:15).

Paul said, "Yea, and if **I be offered** upon the sacrifice and service of your faith, I **joy, and rejoice** with you all" (Phil. 2:17).

Paul said, "And ye became followers of us, and of the Lord, having **received the word in much affliction, with joy** of the Holy Ghost" (I Thess. 1:6).

Peter said, "Beloved, think it not strange concerning **the fiery trial which is to try you**, as though some strange thing happened unto you: But **rejoice**, inasmuch as ye are partakers of Christ's sufferings; that, when his glory shall be revealed, ye may be **glad** also with exceeding **joy**" (I Pet. 4:12-13).

Jesus said, "**Blessed** are ye, when men shall **revile** you, and **persecute** you, and shall say all manner of evil against you falsely, for my sake. **Rejoice**, and be exceeding **glad**: for great is your reward in heaven" (Matt. 5:11-12).

When (and only when) we know the fellowship of His sufferings on a personal and intimate level, we will come to know the power of His resurrection. When we begin to experience that pain, we know that it is time to get up out of the tomb. We are ready to walk in the Spirit, because we now know His resurrection power.

Only after experiencing that resurrection power do we have His power to face our battles. Many of us face our battles alone, relying on our own strength and power. It's no wonder that so many Christians are living defeated lives. If the archangel Michael needed God's power to defeat Satan (Jude 9), what on earth makes us think we can defeat the enemy on our own? Every battle we fight in His power brings victory; every battle we fight on our own brings defeat.

Resurrection brings you a new life. This resurrection is a great blessing, for it is the result of God being granted greater access to control our lives. Many people are looking for that "second blessing." A second blessing is not your getting more of the Holy Spirit; it is the Holy Spirit getting more of you. When we die, He can live in and through us. When I decrease, He increases (John 3:30).

When the great evangelist D. L. Moody was alive, he was known as a man who walked in the power of the Holy Spirit in an unusual way. Once a group of pastors was meeting to consider inviting Moody to come and preach a revival in their town. After listening to these men sing Moody's praises for awhile, one pastor got fed up. He said, "You men talk like Moody has a monopoly on God." One wise pastor responded, "No, God has a monopoly on Moody!" That is what the resurrection Christian lifestyle looks like in practice.

The victorious, successful, rejoicing Christian life is not just about being saved; it is about walking in the Spirit. Only in His power can we love God and love others. In order to gain His power, we must "know Him and the power of His resurrection." This intimacy in knowledge comes from the "fellowship of His sufferings." That intimate familiarity comes from being made conformable to His death. It's this simple: know pain—know gain! That is the purpose of God's "University of Adversity." This is not a school of religion. It's a school of relationship.

FELLOWSHIP
HOW WE *ENJOY* GOD

"Not forsaking the assembling of ourselves together, as the manner of some is; but exhorting one another: and so much the more, as ye see the day approaching."
– Hebrews 10:25

Fellowship is learning to enjoy God by joining with His people and spending time with them. Many Christians fall into the trap of thinking the pastor tells them to come to church just so the building will be full and the offerings will be better. But God has created us as a family unit to need each other. By fellowship, we both give and receive encouragement to help us live victoriously. Fellowship with other believers is an essential ingredient of victory.

FELLOWSHIP IS ENTERTAINMENT WITH GOD'S PEOPLE.

I explain the danger of bad fellowship with the wrong people in my book, <u>Umbrella Fella'</u>. In <u>Umbrella Fella'</u>, I explain how the influence of bad friends is deadly. That's why Psalm 1 warns us about the counsel of the ungodly, the way of sinners, and the seat of the scornful. Using excerpts from this book, I will explain how I learned this danger firsthand in my own life.

I grew up in a neighborhood that had multiple kids my age who attended my Christian school. But in my teen years, I began to choose after-school friends in the neighborhood who did wrong. It wasn't that they were extremely wicked, it was just that they did wrong. At first I only played neighborhood sports with them—baseball, football, riding around on our bikes. But eventually I was old enough to drive. I would go where they went, and I would sometimes do the things they would do. I was in their *way*, and they eventually got in God's way.

Though we just "hung around" so to speak, eventually these young boys became young men. I can still remember the first time I was faced with something that was obviously sin for it was something that was obviously against every essence of my umbrella of protection (my parents, preachers, teachers, employer, and our government). It was the summer of my 17th birthday. My next door neighbor was fifteen and he was a wrong-doer. He was critical of authority and disobedient to his parents. We played ball together and became good friends.

But that summer, he went to visit his cousin in St. Louis, Missouri. While he was there, my young friend was introduced to marijuana by his uncle. Upon his return home from summer vacation, my friend brought some home to share with his friends. I remember that day when I walked into my friend's garage and he was lying on a discarded mattress. He was smoking what looked to be a strange looking cigarette. My friend had picked up smoking cigarettes six months earlier, and with my being in his "way," I had already smoked a few myself. My curiosity led me to try his marijuana cigarette. In five minutes' time I had rejected every authority in my life: the rules of my parents, the sermons of my preacher, the lessons of my teachers, the policies of my employer, and the laws of my government.

In my senior year, things only got worse. The school enrollment was declining, and many of my old friends didn't come back that fall. But a new student, who was quite enjoyable to hang around, joined my class. He was friendly, funny, and a lot like me. We became fast friends. However, he had had a troubled past and was attending our school after having spent a few years in reform school. Of course, a young man like that would surely struggle with authority, and he did; not only on the outside, but on the inside.

Since I appeared to others to be a submissive student and was thought to be a fine Christian young man, many of our school teachers and staff assumed I would be a good influence on my new friend. However a good apple can never turn a rotten one good. Rather one bad apple can turn a whole bushel bad. My friend had the boldness to defy authority externally in a way that I only wished I could. He always seemed to get away with it!

As my friend would act out his bitterness toward

his boundaries of authority, I soon followed suit. However, I knew how to perform for my teachers. I was careful and allowed my criticism to come out only to those whom I had befriended. I found great delight in convincing my fellow schoolmates to take my position as a scorner. What in the world had happened to me? I had allowed wrong **fellowship** to influence me to follow wrong attitudes with wrong behavior. It was nearly twenty years later before I finally realized my sin and repented.

When I came back to Christ in 1993, one of the things I did wrong was to try to maintain fellowship with those who did not love the Lord. At Reformers Unanimous, we teach in Principle #6 that "those who do not love the Lord will not help you serve the Lord."

As a returning, wayward child, I did not have any good friends yet, and there were not many people my age in the church. I did not consider being alone an option, so I kept a foot in both puddles, so to speak. I would go to all three services each week and even a singles activity once in a while. But during the week and on some weekend evenings I would hang out with my old friends. I would commit to do right, but was always led to do wrong.

I played in an indoor sand volleyball league with some of those friends. Every Sunday evening, after a wonderful day at church, I would head off to the sports arena to play our league games. My goal was to play the games, enjoy my friends and excuse myself before they went to the club at the back of the courts. Every week I committed that I would not attend the club activities after the games. My friends who knew I was trying to quit drinking would compel me to come along by saying, "C'mon! You can just drink soda. It's no fun without you!"

Remember—this was not just their wish; this was their counsel. Week after week I failed, but week after week they would counsel me to try it again. This was ungodly counsel and it stunted my growth for the first three months that I attended church.

Finally, I was invited to an all night church activity on New Years' Eve. At the same time, these old friends invited me to attend a party with some of them and be their designated driver. They counseled me that if I did not drive for them, I would leave them in a vulnerable position. I had a decision to make. I chose to follow the leading of the Spirit and attend the church activity. If I had not listened to Him that night, I very likely would still be an addict today.

After staying up all night and having an absolute blast with the new friends I was meeting at church, my life was forever changed during my short drive home that New Years' Day morning.

As I drove to my home, weary and worn from an all night fellowship with those who loved God, I was stopped at a red light at a prominent intersection near our church. While waiting at that intersection, I saw my old friends drive by on their way home from that party. I realized immediately that this was not a coincidence. This was a very strong message from God. I "listened" carefully to what I "saw."

On the faces of my friends I could see the misery of a night of ingesting illegal drugs and excessive drinking. They were living in sin, and I had spent my evening wonderfully secure in Him! That day I decided to walk in the counsel of the godly and made my preacher, my teachers, my parents, and my employer my counselors. They have never steered me away from Christ.

However even though I was back in church and committed to having the right kind of friends, I still made a big mistake. My mistake was that, as I began to make new friends in church, I neglected to determine whether they were walking in godly counsel or whether they were standing in Christ, or, if by being with them, I would still be standing in the way of sinners. I just assumed that if they were going to church instead of the bar that they would be a positive influence on me.

As I began attending functions with the singles Sunday school class, I started to meet some fine people who were younger than me. They were in their early twenties and I was twenty-eight. However there was a huge gap: they were an innocent twenty and I was a very exposed twenty-eight.

It was an exciting time in my life because these new friends were people who would not even consider doing the things I had done. These young people had never dabbled with the unrighteousness that I had fallen into. However, it was not because these Christian school graduates had remained in Christ themselves. Rather they had found perfect happiness within themselves. They were not tempted with unrighteousness, for they had found contentment in their own self righteousness.

So even though these young people were **doing many right things,** they were **not doing things right.** The right that they did, they did within their own power. That is self righteousness. It is *you* doing right; absent of the power and influence of Christ. And it is no substitute for true righteousness. When we are self righteous, we are not abiding in Him; we are abiding in self. When we abide anywhere but in Christ then we are by default abiding in sin... and if you spend your time around people who are abiding in sin, they will bring you down.

What I had to learn was that just because someone was at the church, that didn't mean they were a source of godly fellowship. I could be led astray by people in a Sunday school classroom just as I could by people in a bar. This is being led to different kinds of wrongdoing, perhaps, but led to wrongdoing nonetheless. The people with whom you fellowship are either leading you closer to God or further away from Him—no exceptions.

In order to truly develop ourselves to withstand the shells of sin in the battles of life, we need to be busy. We need accountability. We need to be invested in by others and we need to be investing in others. All of these steps are met and more when we accept our responsibility for fellowship.

I encourage you as new believer or a teacher of believers to choose your friends wisely. Those who love God will help you serve God. Everyone needs friends. But in the Christian life, your friends also need you.

God taught us through the Apostle Paul that relationships and fellowships with people need to be carefully crafted and grafted. When we transition from the world into the Lord's family, we must teach our students, and we ourselves, must be careful to prune off bad fellowships and graft in good relationships. In II Corinthians 6:14 we read, "Be ye not unequally yoked together with unbelievers: for what fellowship hath righteousness with unrighteousness? and what communion hath light with darkness?"

To be yoked is to be a partner with another. We ought never to develop partnerships that fellowship with unbelievers. They will need to be purged from our free time. We need to embrace new friendships of fellowship with those who seek to live sober, righteous and godly lives. This step cannot be overemphasized.

The word *fellowship* is best defined as "two fellows in a ship." If you are building a battleship and have partnered with fellows of ill repute, your ship will be vulnerable. The reason piracy never lasted as an effective way of life is because no one could ever trust the other "fellows on the ship." If you are hanging with wrong doers, how are you going to withstand the one who controls them?

Your ship will be sunk if you reject your ship's need for fellowship with other friendly ships in the sea. The more friendly ships you choose to sail the seas of this Christian life the larger will be your fellow "ships." Eventually your fellowship will become a fleet! Who can withstand a fleet of ships dedicated to sailing safely for their Savior?

Teachers and students—fellowship! As a matter of fact, teachers, join your students in fellowship. Students, be open to doing the same. At RU, we strongly encourage our chapter directors to spend at least one meal and three phone calls per week in fellowship with their students. We encourage our RU leaders, who serve the individual students in their challenge groups, to fellowship for at least one meal and two phone calls per week AND to fellowship whenever calls made to them by their students. Friendships need fellowship in order to become relationships.

FOLLOWSHIP
HOW WE *FIND* GOD

"Be ye followers of me, even as I also am of Christ. Now I praise you, brethren, that ye remember me in all things, and keep the ordinances, as I delivered them to you." **-I Corinthians 11:1 & 2**

Followship—being obedient to those God has placed over us—is how we get to God. The Bible refers to the Christian life as a walk; one step does not make a walk, it is instead an ongoing process. To help us walk rightly, God gives us His Holy Spirit. In addition to that inward persuasion, He gives us the outside persuasion of God-ordained authority.

FOLLOWSHIP IS GETTING BEHIND GOD'S LEADERS.

I have found that God leads through authority, especially for children, either physically or spiritually. I was not aware of this truth growing up in a Christian home and school. I thought that authority was there to set rules that I should obey, but I did not know authority was intended by God to be representatives, like the Spirit, of the voice of God.

The summer after my senior year of high school, I did not have enough money to go to Bible college. So I decided that I would stay home for a semester. Just one semester at home to save some money was my intent. As a "just turned" 18 year-old young man, I was surprised that my parents strongly disagreed when I "told" them I would sit out one semester. But they were not the only ones to disagree with my poor decision. My preacher suggested I go, my teachers suggested I go. Even my employer made it possible for me to go through a transfer to that region of the United States.

To be honest with you, I knew that I was probably making the wrong decision. That perception came from His Holy Spirit living within my spirit. But I rejected it all for what I thought was a better plan— save money so that I could be in a stronger position the next semester.

Of course my decision was unwise, but not

because going to college with money is much wiser. Rather, it was unwise because it was in direct disobedience to the wishes of God and of His ordained authority in my life. This decision was made easy by the fact that I could not clearly discern the voice of God. Why? It was because Christ was in me, but I was not in Christ.

I was not surrounded by His limits. His Spirit and His leaders over me all spoke the will of God. But I would not follow, for I was walking after the desires of my flesh. My plan was good, but it wasn't God's plan. This is how the devil has always worked. He has always used outside pressure or circumstances to try to get us to reject the internal voice of God or the external persuasion of our leadership. He has done it every time he has manifested himself to mankind. My decision to reject the counsel of God's authorities took me far away from Him.

As I look back on my life now, I can clearly see that I was unaware of the value of my umbrella of protection (again, my parents, preachers, teachers, employer and government). In my book Umbrella Fella I explain in detail this term "umbrella of protection". Using some of the truths of this book, I would like to help you better understand God's "system: of managing us, through God ordained, Spirit led followship.

Let's begin with one simple requirement God places on young people to ensure they develop early aged followship. "Children, obey your parents in all things: for this is well pleasing unto the Lord." Colossians 3:20

I realize this verse is speaking of the parent/child relationship, but let's look at the greater picture as it applies to obedience. God's intention for a child is to obey His parents through followship. The parents also lend their authority to the child's teachers, their pastor, and other institutions for the benefit of the child. When the child disobeys any form of leadership that the parents have put over him, then he has disobeyed his own parents. He is not following. He is going his own way. This displeases God. He wants children to obey in all things.

Why is God concerned about a child's obedience to every form of authority? It is quite simple. God has ordained a system. It is called "God's system of management". God's system of management is made up of leadership that is intended to help us make good decisions. This leadership begins with our parents. God is pleased when we obey our parents because we are learning the importance of obedience as children. If this principle is learned, especially at a young age, we will develop properly under God's system of management because we will likely continue to follow God's ordained leadership throughout our lives. Most of us, of course, failed to learn this principle as children. We are learning it as adults. And it must be learned! We will never build better battleships for battle until we teach ourselves and the ships we build to obey.

Beginning in childhood, God uses authority to help us choose properly in these four key areas of our lives. Unfortunately, many of us did not follow God's system. As a result, our marriages are not what they should be, our careers are more like jobs, we can't seem to get ahead financially, and we have not placed any priority on our walk with God. Life seems to have no real meaning or purpose. Why has this happened? Because we did not please God with our lives. We cannot expect God to bless our lives if we are not pleasing Him. Obeying authority in all forms and in all things is what pleases God.

So how do we correct our errors? It may be simple for me to explain, but make no mistake, it will be hard to follow. You see, God's intention for a child to obey his parents is so that the child may learn at a young age to submit to authority. God intends for this submission to be carried over to other forms of authority as the child grows and matures. If we did not learn to submit to authority early in life, then we have probably become somewhat resistant toward most authority. Our lifetime of resistance to followship makes learning this lesson as an adult not only humbling, but difficult as well. However, if we will learn it, we can be sure that God can do for us the very same things that He intended to do for us since childhood. As we submit to God's ordained authority, we will learn how to develop our relationship with our mate. We will learn how to turn our job into a career that brings honor to our Lord. We will learn principles of submission that will have a positive effect on our income level. We will learn how to properly distribute that income in God's way, a definite strategy that will increase our income. We will learn how to have a dynamic love relationship with Jesus Christ! Why? Because we are following God's system of management. We are obeying authority. That is followship that is evident by our obedience and obedience pleases God.

Let's look at the Bible to determine whom God has chosen for us to follow from childhood through adulthood in His system of management.

1. Parents

Ephesians 6:1 *Children, obey your parents in the Lord: for this is right.*

2. Pastors

I Timothy 3:1-2, 4-5 *This is a true saying, If a man desire the office of a bishop, he desireth a good work. A bishop then must be ... one that ruleth well his own house, having his children in subjection with all gravity; (For if a man know not how to rule his own house, how shall he take care of the church of God?)*

3. Teachers

II Timothy 2:2 *And the things that thou hast heard of me among many witnesses, the same commit thou to faithful men, who shall be able to teach others also.*

4. Employers

Ephesians 6:5-8 *Servants (employees), be obedient to them that are your masters (employers) according to the flesh, with fear and trembling, in singleness of your heart, as unto Christ; Not with eyeservice, as menpleasers (but rather as God-pleasers); but as the servants of Christ, doing the will of God from the heart; With good will doing service, as to the Lord, and not to men: Knowing that whatsoever good thing any man doeth, the same shall he receive of the Lord, whether he be bond or free.*

5. Government

Romans 13:1, 4 *Let every soul be subject unto the higher powers. For there is no power but of God: the powers that be are ordained of God. For he is the minister of God to thee for good.*

Although there are some who will argue against these positions of authority being God-ordained areas requiring our personal followship, I am sure that they are. The Bible says it, and my personal experience in followship proves it. I have learned, albeit the hard way, that God channels blessing through His authorities. When you are living in rebellion to any of the authorities God has put over you, you are out from under God's umbrella of protection. If there is going to be any benefit to your family, job, or income level, it is going to be because you did the work and God is being longsuffering toward you. It will not be because God is doing the work and blessing you.

The word obedience means to perform what is requested and abstain from what is forbidden. Based on this definition, are we performing and abstaining when it comes to God's ordained authority? We may think we are good employees because we show up and maybe even work hard. But look at your company's policy book. What does it say about attitudes toward one another? What does it say about your conversations between coworkers? If you say that their policy book does not cover those issues, then what does God's policy book say?

How about the government? How do you handle your tax burden? The speed limit? I have heard preachers talk with glee about their speeding habits. That's not good followship. That's rebellion to God ordained authority and it does not please God. Obedience through sweetly submissive followship pleases God. We need to get serious about obeying authority if we expect God to get serious about blessing us. He will not bless a disobedient Christian. He only blesses people when He is pleased with them.

When my daughter Charity was about 4 years old, we established Daddy/Daughter date nights on Monday evenings. On one particular Monday, I called her a few times during the morning from work to remind her how excited I was about our date night and that I couldn't wait to see her. At the end of my workday, my wife came to pick me up. With frustration, Lori began to tell me that Charity had awakened from her nap very grumpy and had been disobedient. Although Lori had been consistent with her discipline, Charity had continued to misbehave throughout the day. My heart sank. As a father, I knew I could not reward the bad behavior of a disobedient child. Charity learned that night that disobedience hindered her from receiving something good from her father. Likewise, disobedience will hinder us from receiving something good from our heavenly Father, as well. I am praying that all my children learn this lesson earlier in life than I did. I want them to know that obeying their parents in all things will not only please Mom and Dad, but it will please God even more. We should focus less on "please, God!" and more on pleasing God by submitting to our God given responsibility to followship.

Today I spend as much time as I can under the influence of godly leaders. I watch them, and try to imitate them as they follow Jesus Christ. This is the pattern the Apostle Paul laid out for us. He wrote, "Brethren, be followers together of me, and mark them which walk so as ye have us for an ensample." (Philippians 3:17)

Remember that while the world looks down on followers, God blesses them. Jesus said, "My sheep hear my voice, and I know them, and they follow me." (John 10:27) The ultimate in followship is walking in the footsteps of Jesus, hearing His voice through reading and meditating on His Word and listening to the inward persuasion of the Holy Spirit of God. Nothing can derail you from doing right if you listening to Jesus and following Him.

The reason the twelve men became Disciples of Christ was because they all had one thing in common. They followed Him. When Jesus ascended and the Spirit arrived, thousands of new converts were born as these discipled published the good news of the gospel. Immediately they began to follow the followers of Christ. To follow the right way, it is imperative we find people who really close to Christ, if we are going to follow the right people. Paul said it best when he said "ye followers of me, even as I also of Christ." (I Corinthians 11:1)

Often times, the best person to follow is to follow the one that God used to birth you. Your spiritual father, so to speak. Paul taught the Corinthian believers that even though there were many people they could learn from, they needed to be careful who they followed. He was their spiritual father and he strongly suggested they follow him as a result. He indicated this in a beseeching, which is to say with great zeal when he wrote "For though ye have ten thousand instructors in Christ, yet *have ye* not many fathers: for in Christ Jesus I have begotten you through the gospel. Wherefore I **beseech** you, be ye **followers of me**." (I Corinthians 4:15, 16)

You can't choose your parents. But you can choose your preacher, your teachers, your employers and your friends. Choose wisely but don't reject your spiritual parent any more than you should not reject your physical parents. Paul said it quite the same to the believers in Philippi. ", be followers together of me, and mark them which walk so as ye have us for an example. For many walk, of whom I have told you often, and now tell you even weeping, *that they are* the enemies of the cross of Christ: Whose end *is* destruction, whose God *is their* belly, and *whose* glory *is* in their shame, who mind earthly things.

Now students, please notice his very clear

warning found here. He tells you that those who are the enemies of the cross have a predetermined end and that end is destruction! Many would agree that we ought not follow those who are the enemies of the cross. But who are these enemies? He describes them as people who focus on themselves, who feed their own appetites in life and are dwell on temporal niceties. They are more interested in things that feed their greed for selfish satisfaction then unselfish service for their Savior.

What was Paul saying? He was telling us to "study our teachers and preachers" and be careful whom we follow. If they are more interested in themselves than in others (that is the cross of Christ), then look to follow someone closer to Christ. Peter said it best when he warned us in I Peter 3:12, 13 that "the eyes of the Lord *are* over the righteous, and his ears *are* ope*n* unto their prayers: **but the face of the Lord *is* against them that do evil.** who *is* he that will harm you, if **ye be followers of that which is good?**

The Hebrew writer wrote that we should "remember them which have the rule over you, who have spoken unto you the word of God: whose faith follow, considering the end of *their* conversation. Notice his encouragement? Follow preachers and teachers whose faith follow them. Does the after acts of those you follow match up with the words spoken in their teaching. Are they talking the talk, but not walking the walk? You should avoid these types of teachers rather than follow them. And when you find one whose faith follows him, than get behind him and "remember them" while also giving them the rule (or leadership) over you. As they lead, you follow and you will see behind you, your faith will follow as well.

Paul told Timothy, "Follow righteousness, faith, charity, peace, **with them** that call on the Lord out of a pure heart. To follow these listed virtues, we will do it best if we do so with others and those others will need to be people of pure mediations who call on the Lord for clear direction in turbulent times.

Though I did not write as many things concerning this portion of our ship building ministry, it should be well noted that nothing will hinder the stability of your battleship than following other ships that lead you improperly in battle.

Want to stay afloat in your boat? Build a better ship through biblically backed followship.

LEADERSHIP
HOW WE GET *TO* GOD

"Behold, I have given [David] for a witness to the people, a leader and commander to the people."
– Isaiah 55:4

Leadership is using the influence God has given us to lead others to Him. Every one of us is a leader in some area—at home, at school, at work, or at church. Our responsibility is to see to it that the influence we have on others is positive, leading them to God instead of away from Him.

LEADERSHIP IS GETTING BEHIND GOD.

When we allow ourselves to be Spirit-led leaders, we get to God. In our followship, we are able to *find* God; through our leadership, we get others *to* Him. God will communicate to us as a leader so we may direct our followship to find Him. In order to find

God, one needs to be under a leader who can get to God. As a leader, you are between God and the followship. God will communicate, guide, direct, lead, and illuminate leadership on behalf of the followship.

Leadership is standing before people with such care and diligence so as to motivate others to get involved in the accomplishment of one's goals. The Bible word for *leadership* is the role of a "ruler." This word *ruler* comes from the Greek word *proistemi* which means "to stand before, to preside, to be over." A leader is a goal setter—someone who has a clear vision for where people need to go and who can get them there!

If we are going to be strong in battle, our ship must not only develop followship behind good leadership, we must develop ourselves for leadership, as well. Inevitably, great followers become great leaders. A great leader is always a great follower.

There are times in every battle where you fight against the enemy with much assistance from your leaders, and sometimes extra help from your followers. But sometimes you will fight alone. At times like that, you must lead yourself properly through the battle, lest you sink your ship in sin.

With that said, you must correctly lead yourself before you can properly lead others. If you are a new believer or a teacher of new believers, you must develop your ship and those ships that follow you. This will require the development of your leader*ship*.

In my book Produce the Juice, I explain how every leader needs to understand the limits of his or her leadership. Leaders need to be careful not to manipulate or coerce others into doing what they want them to do. Jesus condemned this type of leadership. He criticized the Gentile leadership for manipulating people rather than motivating them. "Ye know that they which are accounted to rule over the Gentiles exercise lordship over them; and their great ones exercise authority upon them. But so shall it not be among you" (Mark 10:43-44). Rather, a leader should realize his role and use his gift of persuasion to form a consensus among the people.

I trained under one of the most gifted leaders I have ever met while working in the secular field.

As a young executive in the oil business, I worked for a man named Dan Arnold. He was a gifted motivator. I was Vice President of Operations and Administration over his convenience stores and truck stops.

Under my authority, in the chain of command, were his supervisors. Under them were his managers, and under them were his employees. Yes, they were his supervisors, his managers, and his employees, not mine. All our employees were Mr. Arnold's people. I would see assistant mangers, supervisors, and even myself try just about everything to motivate the staff and often fail. Mr. Arnold was able to succeed with a few carefully chosen words of wisdom. He had the peoples' hearts because he always took the time to build a consensus.

Mr. Arnold was much like the Old Testament leader, Nehemiah. Nehemiah had a heart to see the walls of Jerusalem rebuilt. He was a simple man, the cup bearer for the king, in a position most people would consider to be minor and unimportant. However, God expected Nehemiah to become a leader and he wanted him to do so real fast. I would like to use him as an illustration of how people who feel they are just one of the "little guys" can be used, and often are used, by God to do great things. The reason is because they are willing to develop within their own leadership potential. Let's take a look at the story.

In Nehemiah chapter two, we are introduced to a conversation between the king and his cupbearer, Nehemiah. The king had a lot of respect for Nehemiah and for how well he carried himself in his role of *followship*. As a result, when he saw Nehemiah sad, he knew something had to be wrong. So, he enquired of Nehemiah to find out what was the matter.

Their conversation that day set the stage for one of the greatest projects in the Bible. I believe that during the king's inquisition, Nehemiah came to realize the importance of building a consensus among the people. Without it, a leader will never motivate. Absent of motivation, the leader has only one tool left at his disposal—the dismally dull tool of manipulation.

Let us see how Nehemiah carefully used his

influence to build a consensus, not only with his employer, but also with the governmental leaders of his land, the rulers of other lands, and the people he wanted to help.

"And it came to pass in the month Nisan, in the twentieth year of Artaxerxes the king, that wine was before him: and I took up the wine, and gave it unto the king. Now I had not been before time sad in his presence. Wherefore the king said unto me, Why is thy countenance sad, seeing thou art not sick? this is nothing else but sorrow of heart. Then I was very sore afraid, And said unto the king, Let the king live for ever: why should not my countenance be sad, when the city, the place of my fathers' sepulchres, lieth waste, and the gates thereof are consumed with fire? Then the king said unto me, **For what dost thou make request?**" (Neh. 2:1-4)

At this time, the great leader in Nehemiah was exposed. His response clearly showed his reliance on God and his expectation of God to use the very same people that Nehemiah's leadership qualities had influenced. What was Nehemiah's wise response to the King's question? Nehemiah records his response this way: "So **I prayed** to the God of heaven. **And I said** unto the king…"

He *prayed* to God, but *said* to the king! He knew that God was in control, but he also knew that if God were to meet his need, it would have to be done through the king—the one he had served so faithfully for so many years. So he asked the king to let him go home and rebuild the walls of Jerusalem. The king asked him, "For how long shall thy journey be? and when wilt thou return?" (Neh. 2:6)

The king allowed Nehemiah to go. In fact, he was delighted to do so, as our report details, "So it pleased the king to send me; and I set him a time" (Neh. 2:6). Before he ever left the palace, the leadership and influence of the king was crucial to Nehemiah's goal of rebuilding the walls. He and his people were penniless for this project. He would need a great consensus among the officials that the king had influence over. So he focused his influence on the king in order to get what he needed. He asked the king for more than just permission to go.

"Moreover I said unto the king, If it please the king, let letters be given me to the governors beyond the river, that they may convey me over till I come into Judah; And a letter unto Asaph the keeper of the king's forest, that he may give me timber to make beams for the gates of the palace…, the wall of the city…, and the house that I shall enter into. And the king granted me, **according to the good hand of my God upon me**" (Neh. 2:7&8).

Though Nehemiah was in a position most people would consider far from leadership—a food taster—he carefully used his influence. He faced opposition and attacks, but the work was never hindered or stopped. The consensus Nehemiah built among the people helped them overcome the challenges they faced.

Nehemiah knew the king was helping him do a good work, but he realized that the help he was receiving was the result of "the good hand of God" being upon him! Now he needed some protection. He looked to the king for an army of assistance and the king granted it. "Then I came to the governors beyond the river, and gave them the king's letters. Now the king had sent captains of the army and horsemen with me" (Neh. 2:9).

When Nehemiah arrived, he spent time every evening when no one from the city of Jerusalem was around, viewing the devastation and determining a good plan. He needed a plan around which he could successfully build a consensus and motivate the people to join him. During these initial planning stages, he did not tell anyone what he was doing, not even the rulers of the land. Verse 16 reads, "And the rulers knew not whither I went, or what I did; neither had I as yet told it to the Jews, nor to the priests, nor to the nobles, nor to the rulers, nor to the rest that did the work."

We first see that Nehemiah built a consensus among those over him. He then gained their permission and eventually their support. Finally he gained their provision for his vision. That's an effective consensus from those over you! Now he would begin to build a consensus with those under him as well. Listen to Nehemiah making his first motivational speech to the people. "Then said I unto them, Ye see the distress that we are in, how Jerusalem lieth waste, and the gates thereof are burned with fire: come, and let us build up the wall of Jerusalem, that we be no more a reproach. Then I told them of the hand of my God which was good upon me; as also the king's words that he had spoken unto me." How did the people respond to his motivational words? "And they said, **Let us rise up and build. So they strengthened their hands for this good work**" (Neh. 2:17-18).

The project was soon attacked by four men who were stubbornly against Nehemiah's vision and plan. They ridiculed it and attacked it in every way imaginable. But Nehemiah refused to allow those men to hinder the consensus he was building. Look at his Spirit-led response to these naysayers in Nehemiah 2:20: "Then answered I them, and said unto them, The God of heaven, he will prosper us; therefore we his servants will arise and build."

The Scripture records that "the people had a **mind to work**" (Neh. 4:6). To get "the mind of work" in your people, you must motivate them through consensus, rather than manipulate them through criticism.

As we are required by God to develop our leadership, we must be careful that we balance tasks and people. There can be a tendency to get so caught up in the process that people are overworked and misused. It is one thing to be in a position as a leader where you have to press forward without a consensus. That sometimes happens, and perhaps more often than we would prefer. But at the same time, you don't want to move forward so fast that you give no real thought to the needs of those you are leading.

The Bible gives us a long list of people who misused their leadership and abused their followers. One such person was King Rehobaom. He understood followship, but he never developed his leadership. As a good follower, he was willing to get advice from people. In doing so, he got both good advice and bad advice when he became king following the death of his father, Solomon. But his leadership limitations showed when he took the bad advice and hurt those he had been called to rule. His role as a leader was forever damaged as the kingdom was divided.

The story begins in 1 Kings 12:1. "And Rehoboam went to Shechem: for all Israel were come to Shechem to make him king." At the time of his coronation, some of the people came to him with a request that he ease the tax burden that King Solomon had placed on the people. They said in verse four, "Thy father made our yoke grievous: now therefore make thou the grievous service of thy father, and his heavy yoke which he put upon us, lighter, and we will serve thee."

Having listened to their complaint, he excused them for three days while he thought about their request. During that time, he sought advice from his father's counselors. "And king Rehoboam consulted with the old men, that stood before Solomon his father while he yet lived, and said, how do ye advise that I may answer this people?" (II Kings 12:6)

Those wise men suggested he be a servant to his people and respond positively to their complaint and encourage them. They told him that if he would build a consensus (by answering their questions) and motivate them (by speaking good words) they would follow him faithfully. "And they spake unto him, saying, If thou wilt be a servant unto this people this day, and wilt serve them, **and answer**

them, and **speak good words to them**, then they will be thy servants for ever" (II Kings 12:7). That was wise advice, but Rehoboam also got counsel from some of his peers.

"But he forsook the counsel of the old men, which they had given him, and consulted with the young men that were grown up with him, and which stood before him: And he said unto them, What counsel give ye that we may answer this people, who have spoken to me, saying, Make the yoke which thy father did put upon us lighter? And the young men that were grown up with him spake unto him, saying, Thus shalt thou speak unto this people that spake unto thee, saying, Thy father made our yoke heavy, but make thou it lighter unto us; thus shalt thou say unto them, **My little finger shall be thicker than my father's loins.** And now whereas my father did lade you with a heavy yoke, I will add to your yoke: my father hath chastised you with whips, but I will chastise you with scorpions." (II Kings 2:8-11)

When the people returned on the third day, the mistakes of Solomon and his son Rehoboam came to a head.

"So Jeroboam and all the people came to Rehoboam the third day, as the king had appointed, saying, Come to me again the third day. And the **king answered the people roughly**, and forsook the old men's counsel that they gave him; And spake to them after the counsel of the young men, saying, My father made your yoke heavy, and **I will add to your yoke**: my father also chastised you with whips, but I will chastise you with scorpions." (II Kings 2:12-14)

Rehoboam destroyed the kingdom built up by his father and his grandfather. "So Israel rebelled against the house of David unto this day" (II Kings 12:19). Why did this happen? It was because Rehobaom considered the need for productivity from his people more important than his publicity with the people.

This type of leadership style is rampant in many of our corporations, communities, and sadly even in our churches. I do believe productivity is important, but absent of proper publicity, it makes you a totalitarian leader. By proper publicity, I mean sharing your vision with followers in such a way that they understand it and want to be a part of it.

The man or woman who allows God to develop their battleship to include leadership will lead under the Spirit's influence. The Spirit-led leader considers his influence over his people not as something in which he must lord over them. The biblical pattern for leadership is always servant leadership. Good leadership wants to develop good followship to the point where they can work independently without oversight. It does him no good to lead his people if they are not developing into a self-starting and satisfied work force.

I believe that when we lead under the influence of the Holy Spirit and properly represent a conduit for His true leadership to flow through to the followship He has placed under us, our motives can more easily be trusted and our motivational techniques will be more effective. The reason that most people resist following a leader is because they struggle to trust his motives and do not appreciate his manipulation.

As teachers, we must train our students to develop

their ships for leadership. Our students need to develop in many different areas, and develop them simultaneously. But they arrived under our tutelage already placed in leadership positions in their marriage as husbands, or as a parent or sometimes as employers, or managers of employees. But their leadership, without Christ, has been more oft than not, quite flawed and in need of repair.

The ships we produce at RU are designed early on to be leader-ships; to lead others ships to and through the battle against sin and Satan. Whether you are a new believer or a teacher of new believers, it is important that we design ourselves to include tactical training in leadership. It will be the nautical training we need to navigate the rough waters of the world on behalf of those who are depending on us to stay afloat.

STEWARDSHIP
HOW WE *GIVE* OF GOD'S

"Both riches and honour come of thee, and thou reignest over all; and in thine hand is power and might; and in thine hand it is to make great, and to give strength unto all. Now therefore, our God, we thank thee, and praise thy glorious name. But who am I, and what is my people, that we should be able to offer so willingly after this sort? for all things come of thee, and of thine own have we given thee."
– II Chronicles 29:12-14

Stewardship is our giving of that which *is* God's back *to* God. One of the most important principles the Bible teaches about giving is that everything we have already belongs to God. When we give, we are simply returning to Him that which He already owns. We are managers, not owners, of all that we have. This applies not just to money, but also to our time, influence, talents, and abilities.

STEWARDSHIP IS FUNNELING ON BEHALF OF GOD.

If our ships are to sail safely in seas full of sin, we will need to obtain good stewardship. This importance of this ship is misunderstood. We tend to think that if we are struggling financially, we are unable to be givers or even be good stewards of what we have. Nothing could be farther from the truth. Good stewardship is giving of what God has given to us. He has given us far more than just our money. Our key verse above indicates just some of the things God has given to us to distribute for Him.

In my book, <u>Nevertheless I Live: Living Freely in a Bound World</u>, I biblically expound on God's principles of stewardship. God will lead good people to give of themselves to others, both by way of their money and of their time. We ought to always be willing to give of what God has given to us.

Our key verse uses the phrase "in thine hand." This phrase means "within one's possession and control." These verses are telling us that God is in possession of all these listed things that are of such great value, whether it be riches or promotion, power or might, greatness or strength. These are God's resources that are within His possession and control, and as He provides these things for us, we should offer the same things to others, willingly.

If we are given riches, they come from Him. If we are given honor (promotion), it comes from Him. Power (His authority) and might (physical strength) are gifts of God. Greatness (esteem among men) and strength (ability) are commodities that are given to us by God. Our Second Chronicles passage tells us we should be able to offer so willingly after this sort. Realizing that all these things come from God, we can now willingly offer them back to Him by, under the influence of the Holy Spirit, giving a portion of these resources for the benefit of others. That's good stewardship.

The first gift mentioned is the getting and giving of riches. Getting money is often the beginning of materialism. However, giving away our money will cure any struggle with materialism we may have. Giving is the sure cure for selfishness. A true giver realizes that God ultimately owns everything. Givers find great joy in being trusted by God to distribute His money for the needs of others. Our good stewardship over the riches He has provided will be rewarded with greater riches.

Most people are not satisfied with what God has given to them in the way of money. Have you ever stopped to ask yourself this question, "I wonder if God is satisfied with the money that I have given to others?" Let's not forget God's biblical method for obtaining. It is found in Luke 6:38, "Give, and it shall be given unto you." Before God could commit what we think is a "monetary injustice" to us, we must first have committed a monetary injustice to others. It is that simple. We are the first piece of the equation that unlocks God's treasure chest of riches.

If we will show God we are not materialistic, but rather opportunistic with what we have been given, then what we are given will be increased. This is not a principle—it is a promise! Those who say it is a principle that cannot be counted on are probably poor givers, justifying their self-centered or possession-centered lifestyle. Christ went on to teach in verse 38 of Luke 6 that what is given to us will be returned "good measure, pressed down, and shaken together, and running over (now that's prosperity!), shall men give into your bosom. For with the same measure (determined length) that ye mete (limit) withal it shall be measured to you again." These verses remind us of some basic principles concerning our stewardship of our battleship:

- This verse does not mention money. It is a promise for any given commodity, including money.
- Our giving precedes our getting.
- Our getting is more abundant than our giving—running over (we cannot out-give God).
- Men will be returning your investment—it may not appear to be coming from God.
- The measuring stick that limits our giving will also limit our receiving.

I find one of the best principles that I have learned concerning creating wealth is taught by Jesus in Luke 16:10-14. "He that is faithful in that which is least is faithful also in much: and he that is unjust in the least is unjust also in much. If therefore ye have not been faithful in the unrighteous mammon, who will commit to your trust the true riches? And if ye have not been faithful in that which is another man's, who shall give you that which is your own? No servant can serve two masters: for either he will hate the one, and love the other; or else he will hold to the one, and despise the other. Ye cannot serve God and mammon. And the Pharisees also, who were covetous, heard all these things: and they derided him."

Mammon is a Babylonian term for "money." Jesus is giving us a lesson in stewardship. Steward is an old English word for the modern English word "manager." Thus, Jesus was referring to money management! He told His disciples that if we are unfaithful in the little things, we will be unfaithful concerning larger matters. He then specified one of the little things that people can be unfaithful in stewarding, or managing, money. If we fail to be faithful in managing what is entrusted to us by another, why would that person ever give us anything to keep? Similarly, if we are not giving what we are supposed to be giving, we are not going to be keeping what we hope to be keeping.

Jesus then explained what makes us unfaithful in the distribution of the financial resources that He has given to us to manage. He called it "serving money." "No servant can serve two masters...Ye cannot serve God and mammon (money)." Serving is not the same as slavery. Serving means "to work for." In today's vernacular, the word servant means "employee" (whether paid or volunteer service). So He is teaching us that we cannot be employees of God and employees of our money. Some wealthy people advise, "Don't work for your money; let your money work for you." Jesus is teaching this same financial principle of stewardship. Don't be an employee of your money. Don't let it dictate what you do and how much you get paid for what you do. Rather, serve God. Be an employee of God and let Him determine what you do and how much you get paid for doing it.

Another part of Christ's teaching on money should be noted. Concerning service to two masters, He points out, "for either he will hate the one, and love the other; or else he will hold to the one, and despise the other. Ye cannot serve God and mammon." Based on the order that He listed the two masters (God first and then money), Jesus is teaching us that if we love money, we will hate God. But, if we cling to God, we will despise money. Despise simply means "to have a low opinion of." In other words, loving money will replace our love for God with hatred toward Him. However, if we cling to God as our source of life and prosperity, then we will have a low opinion of money. I have found that when one's opinion of money is in the proper perspective, that person is a giver of it and not a keeper of it. Givers are receivers! God never gives the gift of giving without also giving the gift of earning!

Now for those who may disagree, I offer the final phrase of this passage that Jesus taught His disciples: "And the Pharisees also, who were covetous, heard all these things: and they derided him." The Bible says that those who disagree with this teaching will laugh at it and ridicule it because they are covetous people.

I certainly do not know who God intends to be people of wealth, but I do know this one thing: they will obtain it because they are givers of what He gives them. He will bless their giving with more things to manage as long as they remain givers. This is the best way to compound wealth.

We see in our key verses in Second Chronicles that God also bestows honor upon us that we might willingly offer it to others. Honor is "the promotion of another." It is within God's power to give to us promotion among others. Of course, the pattern for obtaining honor is the same as the pattern for obtaining riches. Give and it shall be given unto you. However, as is the case for wealth, we are tempted to try to obtain our own esteem without first esteeming others. We want to receive without first giving.

As with money, we say, "I would value and respect others if more people would value and respect me!" That's like saying, "I would give more money, if I could get more money first." It doesn't work that way. We must first give in order to receive. The reason we don't like to give in order to receive is because we are not naturally "other people-centered." We tend, in the natural man, to be "self-centered." Our pride stops us from valuing and respecting others without first being valued and respected. The word honor (spelled honour in the King James Version) is found over 135 times in the Bible, and every time it is used, it denotes a submission of some sort. The Bible is clear on this: we will not receive honor from others if we do not give honor. Furthermore, we cannot give honor if we are struggling with self-centered pride. Let's look at a few verses that point this out.

- Proverbs 15:33, "The fear of the LORD is the instruction of wisdom; and before honour is humility."

- Proverbs 18:12, "Before destruction the heart of man is haughty, and before honour is humility."

- Proverbs 22:4, "By humility and the fear of the LORD are riches, and honour, and life."

- Proverbs 29:23, "A man's pride shall bring him low: but honour shall uphold the humble in spirit."

Scripture clearly presents to us that we must humble ourselves before we will be honored. God holds back promotion, or respect and value, from those who are struggling with pride. The Bible cites two things that destroy a man. One makes him fall repeatedly, and the other turns those repeated falls into permanent destruction. They are revealed in Proverbs 16:18. "Pride goeth before destruction, and an haughty spirit before a fall." Pride is "undue esteem; respect or value of oneself." A haughty spirit (otherwise known as arrogance) is "undue contempt for others." In other words, having a low opinion of others will cause a man to fall, and that low opinion of others will eventually lead him to have an unduly high opinion of himself. When that takes place, he will experience destruction in his life. Before we will ever think too highly of ourselves, we will first begin thinking lowly, or less, of others. Consistent falling precedes destruction and arrogance toward others precedes pride in oneself!

We need to be humble. If we will not humble ourselves, God will do it for us. If we will take our focus and place it upon those who are in need of value and respect, we will find ourselves thinking more of them and less of ourselves. Our focus is everything. When it is on us, it leads to pride; when it is on others, it leads to humility that manifests itself in the giving of honor to them.

"But now hath God set the members every one of them in the body, as it hath pleased him. And if they were all one member, where were the body? But now are they many members, yet but one body. And the eye cannot say unto the hand, I have no need of thee: nor again the head to the feet, I have no need of you. Nay, much more those members of the body, which seem to be more feeble, are necessary: And those members of the body, which we think to be less honourable, upon these we bestow more abundant honour; and our uncomely parts have more abundant comeliness. For our comely parts have no need: but God hath tempered the body together, having given more abundant honour to that part which lacked: That there should be no schism in the body; but that the members should have the same care one for another. And whether one member suffer, all the members suffer with it; or one member be honoured, all the members rejoice with it. Now ye are the body of Christ, and members in particular" (1 Corinthians 12:18-27).

Here we see God giving honor to someone who lacked honor. He tells us to do likewise. Those who lack honor, or respect, esteem, and value, are the people who are less comely or less desirable in our eyes. He says that we will think that such people are less honorable, yet these are the people to whom God gives honor. He tells us to not only give them honor, but also to give them "abundant honor." The need for honor is greatest among those who are less desirable. This is so against our human nature, yet it is God's nature. In His power, under His influence, we will give honor to whom honor is due.

This type of honoring of others will produce humility in our own hearts and lives. God will unleash His honor upon the humble. He promises to do it. Give and it shall be given unto you. It is in God's hand to give honor and He gives it to those who willingly give it to others.

God gives us power so that we may give power. Power is defined as "authority." God is the giver of this commodity as well. Good stewardship will value this commodity and distribute it willingly as led by God. Authority is given by God to those who have demonstrated they can handle authority. We call them "leaders." Leaders are usually leaders because they were first and still are good followers. The same principle of giving and getting applies to this gift from God, too. As we yield (which is a form of giving that is within our power) to our God-ordained authority, God will cause others to yield to our ordained leadership.

As an employer, I have found over the years that the best people to advance within my organizations, both in the secular world and in ministry, have been those people who yield to authority. Quite simply, give ground and you will get ground. No one wants employees who resist direction from those in authority over them. As a result, those who resist authority are seldom allowed to rise up the chain of command because of that resistance. Have you ever wondered why those with less talent than you were able to rise higher in the company? Wonder no more! They gave respect to their authorities, and their authorities gave it back to them. To get power, we must yield to those in power. It is that simple. It may sound wrong to worldly thinking, but according to God it is right. Let's see what Scripture has to say about how God distributes His mighty power:

- All power belongs to God. "God hath spoken once; twice have I heard this; that power belongeth unto God" (Psalm 62:11).

- God alone can give power. "...the God of Israel is he that giveth...power unto his people. Blessed be God" (Psalm 68:35).

- God chose to give all His power to His submitted Son. And Jesus came and spake unto them, saying, "All power is given unto me in heaven and in earth" (Matthew 28:18).

- God gave us the power to become sons of God if we have received Him. "But as many as received him, to them gave he power to become the sons of God, even to them that believe on his name" (John 1:12).

- This power is made available through God in us. "But ye shall receive power, after that the Holy Ghost is come upon you…" (Acts 1:8).

- We are powerless without God. "I am the vine, ye are the branches: He that abideth in me, and I in him, the same bringeth forth much fruit: for without me ye can do nothing." (John 15:5).

These verses simply remind us that all power belongs to God; we are powerless. He can give us power, but His giving is based on our willingness to submit to Him. Jesus illustrates this truth for us through His own submission. He was given all the power that belonged to God. This same power is available to the submitted believer. The power available to us is not only the power to become a child of God, but to have access to the power given to Christ as we submit to Him Who is in us—the Holy Ghost. What an amazing truth!

You <u>are</u> under the power of someone. Everyone is. No one is a power unto himself. You are under someone. As a matter of fact, if it is not God, it is the devil. We read in Acts 26:18 the very reason why God sent His only begotten Son: "To open their eyes, and to turn them from darkness to light, and from the power of Satan unto God, that they may receive forgiveness of sins, and inheritance among them which are sanctified by faith that is in me." God's plan has always been to redeem man from the power of Satan unto the power of God. God has all authority; He gave it to His Son, Jesus. It is available for our use, as children of God, submitted to the One who now holds that power, that authority. Psalm 106:8 reads, "Nevertheless he saved them for his name's sake, that he might make his mighty power to be known."

God gives us power as we give, or, yield, to those in power over us. Ephesians 3:20-21 reads, "Now unto him that is able to do exceeding abundantly above all that we ask or think, according to the power that worketh in us, Unto him be glory in the church by Christ Jesus throughout all ages, world without end. Amen."

Many of the words found in our key verses in 1 Chronicles 29 seem synonymous. In some ways they are the same, such as power, might, and strength. But there are also some basic differences. The differences are not so much in the getting of the commodity, as they are in the giving of the commodity. The process of turning our getting into giving is the process of stewardship. It is your ship being a good steward of what God has sent! The next word in our key verse is the getting and giving, under our responsibility of good stewardship of "might." Might is defined as "physical strength;" the physical strength necessary to perform a function. God gives this to us and we then are in a position to *give willingly after this sort*. Again, the same principle as before applies. To get strength, we must give strength. Give, and it shall be given unto you.

Have you ever been low on physical strength? It is times like that when we are incredibly dependent on God. We need God to increase our strength when we are faint. In Isaiah 40:29 we read, "He giveth power to the faint; and to them that have no might he increaseth strength." He goes on to say that even young men will faint and fall as a result of their lack of physical strength. In verse 28, we read that God is the Creator of the ends of the earth and

He doesn't faint, nor is He ever weary. Then, in verse 31, He goes on to tell us how to gain this physical strength from our Lord at our times of urgent need: "But they that wait upon the LORD shall renew their strength; they shall mount up with wings as eagles; they shall run, and not be weary; and they shall walk, and not faint."

This is a very popular verse, but I believe it is often misunderstood. I have heard people explain this verse to mean that we must sit patiently and "wait," and then God will give us what we need so that we may mount up, walk, and run without a loss of physical strength or might. But that interpretation would be against God's nature. It is not that God doesn't tell us to "wait" at times, because He does. Rather, it is that God does not give anything to us, including physical strength, unless we first give it ourselves. (Give, and it shall be given unto you.)

Realizing this truth, I interpret this verse just a bit differently. We see that the person who is waiting on the Lord is already walking and running, albeit wearily and fainting. I highly doubt God is talking about someone who is sitting and "waiting."

Instead, I believe that God gives physical strength to those who "wait" on Him like a waiter waits on us at a restaurant. Have you experienced a bad waiter before? Of course you have. He is not waiting on you; you're waiting on him. He is not serving. He is not there to please. He is focused on too many other things. He is slow and impatient with you. That is a poor waiter. God is looking for a good waiter; one that does not make Him wait to place an order. He wants a waiter who quickly runs to His side, taking His order and filling it. He wants one who serves— with a smile! He realizes that if he "waits" on the Customer properly, he will receive a good tip. That motivates his good service to the Customer.

If we want strength (or might), we must give our strength to God. We must wait upon Him rather than waiting for Him.

I found this truth to be evident in my own life. As a younger Christian, I struggled to give God enough time. I would get up for work without giving Him any time in my morning. I would work hard all day and come home dog-tired. I would try to take care of a few things around the house. I then would spend time with my wife and kids, and by the time I wound down from the day, I was too tired to do anything for others or even catch up on my "God and I" time that I had skipped that morning. I always seemed sapped of my energy to do anything with God or for God, much less for others. I found this a frustrating way to live. It did not seem to be the abundant Christian life; it was more like the redundant Christian life. God was not giving me any might or strength, as I was not giving Him, or others for that matter, any of my might or strength.

I decided to make a change. Reading our verse that states, Give, and it shall be given unto you, I came to suspect it had to do with more than just monetary resources. Maybe it could include physical resources like strength and time. If I gave God more of my energy and time through good stewardship, maybe God would give me more energy or time, or at least make me more productive and happy with my productivity.

To this end, I began to study my Bible and found that God has given the following admonitions in Scripture:

- Ten percent of what God gives (first fruits, or gross amount) should be given back to Him. I decided to give God the first ten percent of my time per week. That would be seventeen hours. I did that by making the following commitments that no other opportunity would take priority over:

- One hour of "God and I" time every morning—first thing in the morning. This equaled seven hours of my time. (The RUI *"It's Personal"* Daily Journal was designed to help me meet this commitment. As a result, I have never struggled to fill a full hour.)

- Church Services. I would attend Sunday School, AM, PM service, Mid-week service, and RU class on Friday. This equaled ten hours of time. Worship would be the "fuel" that my service to others would burn! (7+10=17 hrs. given to God.)

- Six days shall a man work. I decided I would work no more than six days per week for no more than fifty hours in a week. That's five days for "the man" and one for the "wo-man," so to speak. I would work for my employer during the week and around the house on weekends no more than fifty hours total in a week.

- Family time and time invested in others.

I could not find anywhere in the Bible that discussed time commitments to family, but I saw indications such as "we should love our neighbors as ourselves" and we must "hate [family] and serve God and others" (See Luke 14:26). If this latter admonition is not to be taken literally, then at least we can be sure that it means that family should not overrule our commitment to God and others. Thus to be a better steward:

- I would spend twenty hours with my wife and children, uninterrupted, every week.

- I would spend twenty hours serving others. This would show God that I love others as much as I love my family.

- I would serve others and attend services with my family so that I could add extra time to the twenty hours I was spending with them and teach them the value of worship and service, as well.

- That would leave about sixty hours a week to do with as I pleased. I decided I would try my best to get eight hours of sleep per night (fifty-six hours) and spend the rest of the time in preparation and transportation. Thus, if I needed to adjust anything, I would do it in this order:

  1. I would never steal time from God for work, family, others, or sleep.
  2. I would never steal time from work for family, others, or sleep.
  3. I would never steal time from family for others, or sleep.
  4. I would never steal time from others for sleep.
  5. To spend more time on any of the above, I would have to steal time from my sleep.

When I chose stewardship over every minute in my life, my life changed dramatically. From that point on, I found I had the strength and the time to carry out my responsibilities to God, my employer, my family, and to others that I had never had before. It was incredible! It was like I was a new man. Before, I would retire to bed feeling half-dead and wake up (running late for work) frustrated and discouraged in my Christian life. After these commitments kicked in (and after much attack from the enemy to get me to compromise), I found myself going to bed feeling half-dead and waking up rested and excited for the day. But best of all, from that day forward I have experienced a level of productivity in my personal and professional life that I never thought possible.

I had never been an incredibly productive person, but I must say, it is the one thing I receive more compliments on than anything else. God did that! Why? Because I first gave to Him *willingly after this sort* of my strength, and He returned to me renewed strength. God is the One who led me to do this. My soul did not want to give first. It wants, thinks, and feels it should receive before giving. God is not this way. He wants, thinks, and feels that we should give first. That is good stewardship of my battleship. He promises to give us the strength to do this. He says in 2 Corinthians 4:16, "For which cause we faint not; but though our outward man perish, yet the inward man is renewed day by day." If you serve in your own power, you will be faint and feel frustrated and fleshly every new day. If you serve in God's power, His Spirit will do the work—you will be renewed, every day, brand new!

In our key verses in First Chronicles, we are told, "it is in thine hand…to make great." The phrase to make great means "to bring an advance upon one." Literally, it means to advance someone in life. As with all the other commodities that God is able to offer, the power of advancement is not found in getting, but in giving. Yes, as we learn to discern good stewardship we will be able to *offer willingly after this sort*, as well.

Society has taught us that to get ahead in life, we have to look out for number one. Actually, biblically speaking, we need to look out for Number One and Number Two to get ahead in life. The problem is that most people fail to understand whom God considers to be Number One and Number Two. Number One is to love God with all your heart, soul, and mind; and Number Two is to love others as yourself. These two commandments are the cornerstone of Christian behavior. Under our own influence, we will struggle to meet either command. Under the influence of the Spirit, we will fulfill them both. Esteeming others is the best way, the only way to get ahead in life—to advance.

I think the verses in the Bible that best define the pathway to personal and professional success are found in Philippians 2:3-11. "Let nothing be done through strife or vainglory; but in lowliness of mind let each esteem other better than themselves. Look not every man on his own things, but every man also on the things of others. Let this mind be in you, which was also in Christ Jesus: Who, being in the form of God, thought it not robbery to be equal with God: But made himself of no reputation, and took upon him the form of a servant, and was made in the likeness of men: And being found in fashion as a man, he humbled himself, and became obedient unto death, even the death of the cross. Wherefore God also hath highly exalted him, and given him a name which is above every name: That at the name of Jesus every knee should bow, of things in heaven, and things in earth, and things under the earth; And that every tongue should confess that Jesus Christ is Lord, to the glory of God the Father."

Now that's a success story of good stewardship! From a servant to being highly exalted with a name that would cause people to bow! Let's look at the key ingredients of Christ's success:

- He did not seek to cause contention among others.

- He realized it was a waste of time (vain) to make Himself look good (glory).

- He was humble (lowly) and considered (esteemed) the needs of others.

- He did not focus on His reputation as God, but on His opportunity to serve as a man.

- He sacrificed His life to meet the needs of others.

As a result of His good stewardship of what God had given Him, the Bible tells us that God exalted Him. It is within God's power to "make great." And He did! He made Jesus the greatest name in all the earth! He made Him King of kings and Lord of lords! The day will come when every knee will bow at the feet of this great God who became a Servant. Jesus loved God enough to serve others. He became the two commandments personified,

I was never a leader in life. I was always a follower. If you were to see a story of my life, you would see a young man overshadowed by his much more talented siblings. You would see a boy who struggled to get through school, being held back a year once and almost help back a second time. I was a boy who was "void of understanding." I knew everything there was to know about God, but I did not know God. He knew me and I was going to Heaven, but my relationship with Him as a young, Christian school graduate was weak. As a result, I was vulnerable to the tempter. I found myself getting further and further from God.

As a follower, I strayed from my good friends and found more "exciting" bad friends. These friends led me into the paths of unrighteousness and I eagerly followed. Being a follower, I could not and would not lead anyone, especially to the path of righteousness. After ten years of rebellion against God, I looked back and saw the devastation of my life. I was a drug addict, deeply in debt, homeless, and out of work. I had lost several good jobs. My résumé was so bad that I could not find a job without outright lying to the potential employer about my previous employers. It was a pitiful place to be, far from what I had hoped my life to become and I was desperately in need of God to intervene. I just wanted "a life" and wasn't looking for God to make it great. I just assumed that was impossible.

However, my testimony, taught in the book <u>Tall Law: When Trying Hard Isn't Good Enough</u>, reveals that through a serious car accident, God got my attention. I started going back to church and was given time to grow and mature a little before being offered an opportunity to serve in a ministry. When I did finally begin to help others, something began to change in my life. I started to really enjoy giving of my time and energies to others. It made me feel as good as living for myself had made me feel bad. I hate to say it, but I became addicted to serving others.

Almost immediately, God gave me a job at a

machine shop making $6/ hour. He was beginning to bless me as I gave of myself willingly. I continued to serve others with a passion, and God gave me a fiancée and a $10/ hour job. My passion then became souls. Not just serving people, but reaching people for Christ. I married and my pay rose to $13/ hour, though I had no training in machine shop work, just a good attitude and a servant's spirit.

Shortly thereafter, God put it upon my heart to start a Bible study for addicts called Reformers Unanimous. I began to minister to them on Friday nights. My phone rang one night shortly thereafter. "Are you saved?" was the first phrase I heard. "Yes," I replied. "Praise the Lord," was the response of the caller. It was a former employer who I had worked for during my years of addiction. He owned some convenience stores and had been saved through reading my testimony in an RU tract that had been passed on to him! He decided to call and offer me employment.

For the next five years, I went on a ride that, to this day, I find nearly impossible to believe. In year one, our addictions class averaged thirty students, and I earned $30,000 that year. God removed my debt in one year, and my wife and I spent nearly all our time serving others. In year two, I moved up to General Manager and $56,000 annually, as RU doubled to sixty students per week. In year three, RU doubled again to over 120 students every week, as I daily spent from 4:30-6:30 AM writing what would later be our program curriculum. At the same time, I was promoted to Vice President of Operations and later of Administration, making a six figure income.

I am here to tell you that it was within God's power to make great, not mine. Everything I had done with my life on my own ended up in destruction. After five years of business and ministry, my pastor suggested that I enter the ministry of Reformers full time. A month later, though at first unwilling, my employer agreed. I jumped from being a junior executive to being a full time servant, making just over $12,000 my first year in ministry. I never could have planned nor done all that on my own. Never! God showed me that it is within His power to "make great."

Good stewardship over what God gives is the best way to get ahead. And the best way to get ahead is to put others ahead of you. To get God to make you great, you must *give willingly after this sort.* You must make others great, esteeming them more highly than yourself.

Well, we have seen that God is the One who can give riches, honor, power, might, and to make great. He does it for those who first *offer so willingly after this sort.* Remember these verses when placing your gift in the getter's hands: "But this I say, He which soweth sparingly shall reap also sparingly; and he which soweth bountifully shall reap also bountifully. Every man according as he purposeth in his heart, so let him give; not grudgingly, or of necessity: for God loveth a cheerful giver. And God is able to make all grace abound toward you; that ye, always having all sufficiency in all things, may abound to every good work" (II Cor. 9:6-8).

If you give cheerfully (on purpose, without feeling forced) and in abundance to others, you will have all things in sufficiency, and you will abound in every good work. Your steps will be ordered by the Lord and He will lead you to give. After you give, then you will receive. And you will learn the truth Jesus taught, "It is more blessed to give than to receive" (Acts 20:35).

Good stewardship is simply storing what God gives you until He determines how He wants you to distribute it. Everything God made gives. Or shall I say, almost everything. I will conclude our study on stewardship with this poem, author unknown.

GOD MADE—IT GIVES

God made the sun—it gives.
God made the moon—it gives.
God made the stars—they give.
God made the air—it gives.

God made the clouds—they give.
God made the earth—it gives.
God made the sea—it gives.
God made the trees—they give.

God made the flowers—they give.

God made the fowls—they give.
God made the beasts—they give.
God made the plants—they give.

God made man—he took…

If you are a new believer, or a teacher of new believers, you must be committed to equipping your ship with the weapon of stewardship. If you give, even to those who try to harm you, as you are led to do so by the Holy Spirit, God will give to you in return. Good stewardship of our money and time are absolutely imperative to surviving the sea of sin and its many influences. If we will teach our students, and if we will be good students of stewardship, we will see that God will give us more than we could have ever imagined, no matter our income level. He will not only bless us in our money, but also in our productivity and in our performance.

APPRENTICESHIP
HOW WE *SERVE* GOD

"But take diligent heed to do the commandment and the law, which Moses the servant of the Lord charged you, to love the Lord your God and to walk in all his ways, and to keep his commandments, and to cleave unto him, and to serve him with all your heart and with all your soul." **– Joshua 22:5**

Another purpose for our lives on earth is unselfish, service to God. It ranks up there with our first ship—worship. If you loved Him, you would serve Him. If we really loved Him, we would really serve Him. If we wholly loved Him, we would truly serve Him. Get the picture? Our service is a manifestation of our love.

Our ship is not battle ready if it is unwilling to work when commanded by its manufacturer. The Bible tells us in Ephesians 2:10 that we are His "workmanship." It does not say we are His workers; but rather, we are His workmanship. Do you know what the word *workmanship* means? It means "manufactured product." We are not manufacturing a product, for we are not manufacturers at all. We are products *being* manufactured. And when our Saviour, the Master Ship Builder, tells us to set sail, we ought not sit idly by while others in the fleet shove off in selfless service for Him. God would not send us into the stormy seas where sin swims freely without preparing you and me to be fit for service. This preparation of our ship for service is our personal and spiritual apprenticeship.

In the past, young men would work with a master in a trade until they had learned enough to be useful for their master. The word *apprentice* is defined as "one who is bound for a certain time to learn an occupation, in which time his master is equally bound to instruct him."

When Paul trained Timothy to be a servant of the Lord Jesus Christ, it was an apprenticeship. Paul was bound to his God ordained responsibilities and Timothy should have felt an obligation to follow through in his training. As a matter of fact, Paul thought it best that Timothy transition out of his apprenticeship by becoming a master, bound similarly as Paul was to him, to his very own apprenticeship program. He did so as he exhorted him thus: "the things that thou hast heard of me among many witnesses, the same commit thou to faithful men, who shall be able to teach others also" (2 Tim. 2:12).

APPRENTICESHIP IS BECOMING USABLE FOR GOD.

Apprenticeship is God's training program for man. I have learned that there is no service for God that is usable apart from love. Any ship that God will sail into service will anchor and float its boat on love. Yes, God is the true Captain of the "Love Boat!" A ship without love is in no shape to ship anything!. We need masters who feel bound to train us to love one another, even as Christ has loved us. It was His love that led Him to suffer for the sins and sake of another, and it was His suffering that He endured, "leaving us an example that ye should follow in His steps" (I Pet. 2:21).

I feel that if our ship has not been shaped in

order to love, then we will misunderstand the entire reason we remain steadfast in battle. The enemy's entire purpose for fighting us and all other ships in our fleet it to hinder greater manifestations of God's love to hurting people. God loves everybody. The devil does not love anybody, he hates everybody. Jesus died that we might live. The devil lives that we might die. There are no two ways around it, God's love reigns supreme. The devil's battle strategy has always been to thwart the love of God, as expressed through His Son Jesus Christ from being communicated to those sunk in the seas of sin.

As new believers, or teachers of new believers, it is imperative that we and our students understand His love, embrace His love, share His love, and teach others how to do so likewise.

My pastor, Dr. Paul Kingsbury, is my primary trainer. I was his apprentice in love. He loves his family, his wife, his ministry, his church, and his life. His love for His Savior and his love for others sandwiches those other five loves. At the top, His love for Christ is because of Christ's love for him. He has taught me in my apprenticeship program that we ought to love Him because He first loved us and gave Himself for us (I John 4:19).

At the bottom of his love chain is others. His love for Christ trickles through his family, wife, ministry, church, and life to be motivational catalysts of his love for others. In other words, the love of Christ grants Pastor Kingsbury such a healthy emotional stability and prosperity that he wants it to be shared by everybody! That's why my pastor is a good master (teacher, trainer) and that is why I have chosen to be in his apprenticeship program. You should do the same. Find the right person (your pastor, teacher, or counselor) to whom you can be close and that absolutely expresses a daily love for God, and ask them if you could engage in an apprenticeship under them.

But just learning how to serve with your free time will not be enjoyable long term unless you learn to do so out of a heart of genuine love for others that is prompted by Christ's love for you and motivated by the great love you have for those who love life with you. Jesus (the greatest master, teacher, and trainer that ever lived) taught His disciples during their three year apprenticeship program more on the subject of love than all other subjects combined. Though it is seldom taught and caught in our churches today, we see very little evidence of it in Christian service. Our ships are focused more on selfish service for affirmation than sacrificial service for the glory of God.

Notice how Jesus taught His disciples to follow what He had learned in valuable apprenticeship with the Father. "As the Father hath loved me, so have I loved you: **continue ye in my love**" (John 15:9). This is Apprenticeship 101. My father loved me, so I loved you. You do the same!

Love is defined at Reformers Unanimous as "the willing, sacrificial giving of one's self for the benefit of others without thought of return." Self love, which is the highest form of human love, is very similar to Christ's love, but with one glaring exception. *Self-love* is "the willing or unwilling giving of one's self for the benefit of another **with** selfish thoughts of return." In the book <u>Umbrella Fella</u>, we taught the truth that if we continue in His love, we will remain positioned "in Christ." But self love will cost us our position in Christ and place us in sin. Self love is the love that we express as humans to those we care about the most. It is a conditional love, but it is not a positional love. It is the love that most of us have for others, even our spouses.

That is to say, husbands don't mind bringing home the bacon, but we expect our wives to at least cook it for us. That is a willingness to sacrifice for the benefit of your family, but you have thoughts of return. You love her, but you expect her to love you in return. This is self love, and it is a beautiful form of human love. But it is a far cry from the love God wants our ships to set sail, in service holding forth. Our ship must express His love to others as our boat floats gently up and over the waves of wandering sailors.

God's love for us was unconditional and unselfish. It was personified in the life of His Son, but was given with no expectations or demands of anything in return. That is the love submitted to by Jesus when He said that He was in His Father and His Father was in Him. This is the love in which we are to continue. His love is not an exception for us;

it is our expression of Him!

Can you recall before you were saved? You were a person who most likely loved some people. Now that you are saved and God has given you the fruit of the Spirit love, do you think it would be His wish for you to continue to yield to your own form of love? Of course not! Why would He want us to use our flawed love when we have perfect love available to us? It is like jumping out of your broken down battleship and choosing to be the commander in a row boat instead of a tug boat. One requires hard work *by* you; the other does all the work *for* you!

If He wanted us to utilize our own form of love, He would not have placed His love within us. Most assuredly, we ought to yield to His love. Our love may be acceptable to others, but it is unacceptable to Him.

God used the beloved John to portray this truth in his writings more so than any of the other Bible authors. The books of John and First John are full of passages backing up the truth that love is an apprenticeship truth that must be taught, caught, and brought to everyone to whom we interact.

John's apprenticeship under Jesus was so closely intertwined that he received the accolade he was the disciple whom Jesus loved. John really understood what it meant to be loved by Jesus, and as a result of his apprenticeship, he showed that love to Jesus and others. When you can truly relate to how much Jesus loves you, then you will be able to clearly love Him and others. John knew this because He had learned it.

Maybe that is why John was the only disciple who showed up at the crucifixion. Maybe that is why Jesus gave him the responsibility to care for His mother after His death. Maybe that is why John was the only disciple who did not die a martyr's death. Maybe that is why Jesus gave him a special, shall we call it "Revelation" that would conclude God's inspiration through man. Maybe that is why John was the one to proclaim "for God so loved the world that He gave. . ." Maybe that is why John was the only person in Scripture to proudly proclaim that GOD IS LOVE!

Is God just? Yes, He is. Does God chasten? Yes, He does. But, He does all of this because He loves.

For whom the Lord **loves** He chastens. You can say what you want about God, but you cannot get away from the truth that **God is love and man is self-love**! That is why we must die, and He must live. We must decrease, and He must increase.

First John 4 is a beautiful passage that teaches the manifestation of His love. I have placed some language in parenthesis and bolded other portions within these verses for emphasis.

"Beloved, let us **love** one another: for **love** is of God; and every one that **loveth** is born of God, and knoweth God (that's more than just salvation, that's a personal relation!). He that loveth not knoweth not God; for **God is love**. In this was manifested the **love** of God toward us, because that God sent his only begotten Son into the world, that **we might live through him**." – I John 4:7-9

Why did He give us His love? Was it that we might be saved? Was it that we might be forgiven for our sins? Was it that we might lead others to Christ? Was it that we might gain the Holy Spirit? No. Those are all great and glorious byproducts of why God sent His only begotten Son into the world, but they are not the reason. John tells us why God gave us His love in the last portion of verse 9—that we might live through Him. When He lives through us, we must wonder how His life through us will be expressed.

"Herein is **love**, not that we loved God, but that he loved us, and sent his Son *to be* the propitiation for our sins. Beloved, **if God so loved us**, we ought also to **love one another.**" – I John 4:10-11

My friends, that's apprenticeship! As God loved Jesus and Jesus loved us, we also ought to express His love toward others through us. John is saying, in here (herein) is the willing, sacrificial giving of one's self for the benefit of others without thoughts of return: it is found in God's gift of His Son. That is love personified. Below is a verse that will tell us if we are situated in our apprenticeship program.

"No man hath seen God at any time. If we **love** one another, **God dwelleth in us**, and his **love is perfected in us**. Hereby know we that **we dwell in him**, and **he in us**, because he hath given us of his Spirit. And we have seen and do testify that the Father sent the Son *to be* the Savior of the world. Whosoever shall confess that Jesus is the Son of God, **God dwelleth in him**, and he in God (salvation's starting position). And we have known and believed the **love** that God hath to us. God is **love**; and he that **dwelleth in love dwelleth in God, and God in him**." – I John 4:14-16

I am not so sure I could word it any more clearly than John did in these three verses. The apprenticeship of love is, without question, a key ship in developing a battle-ready battleship. Let's manufacture our ship and the ship of those we shape to be vessels of perfection. We will need perfect love to do so:

"**Herein is our love made perfect**, that we may have boldness in the day of judgment: because **as he is, so are we in this world**. There is no fear in love; **but perfect love casteth out fear**: because fear hath torment. **He that feareth is not made perfect in love. We love him**, because **he first loved us**." – I John 4:17-19

We may conclude that before we can love others, we must first have been loved by Him. That's apprenticeship! In our apprenticeship of love, we learn how His love passes through us to others. Our love is useless. It needs to be made perfect. His love is limitless. Oh, that we would take back this cliché to "love others" and embrace it for our own unspeakable joy.

I would like to reveal this KEY Truth to you from the Bible in a deeper and more intimate way. Please remain focused and even prepare yourself in advance to study these next few pages. I believe that what you are about to read could most definitely overwhelm you. It is the secret Truth that remains hidden. It is the KEY to exposing the Hid-N-Life™ to a hard-working, well-meaning, but frustrated Christian shipbuilder.

If you choose just to gloss over these verses, then you might as well close the book and set it down. But if you do, then I believe you could consider a great portion of what you have read to this point to have been a waste of time; for you will miss a KEY to maintaining the buoyancy of your boat.

1. *Truly loving others is an expression **from our Master teacher** through those of us who have joined his apprenticeship:*

- Matthew 5:43-44, "Ye have heard that it hath been said, Thou shalt **love** thy neighbor, and hate thine enemy (that was an Old Testament command). But I say unto you, **Love** your enemies, **bless** them that curse you, **do good** to them that hate you, and **pray** for them which despitefully use you, and persecute you. . ."

- First John 3:11, 14&16, "For this is the message that ye heard from the beginning, that we should **love one another**. . . We know that we have passed from death unto life, because **we love the brethren**. He that loveth not *his* brother abideth in death. . . Hereby **perceive we** the **love of God**, because **he laid down his life for us**: and **we ought to lay down our lives for the brethren.**

- First John 3:23, "And this is his commandment, that we should believe on the name of his Son Jesus Christ, and **love one another**, as he gave us commandment."

I do not know about you, but this kind of love is impossible in my own power, especially toward those that curse, hate, and persecute me! However, in the preceding verses of the above passage in Matthew 5, Jesus claims that He did not come to eliminate this law, but to fulfill it! That means I do not have to love others, He does! All I have to do is LEARN as a personal apprentice to yield to and beautifully express His love rather than my self-righteous self love or my unrighteous hate. Truly loving others can only be done as an expression of Christ's love. We share our apprenticeship with others by loving others.

2. *The law can only be fulfilled as we express Christ's love.*

- Matthew 22:36-40, one asked Jesus, "Master, which *is* the great commandment in the law? Jesus said unto him, Thou shalt **love the Lord** thy God with all thy heart, and with all thy soul, and with all thy mind. This is the first and great commandment. And the second *is* like unto it, Thou shalt **love thy neighbor** as thyself. On these two commandments hang all the law and the prophets."

- Romans 13:8, "Owe no man any thing, but to **love one another**: for he that **loveth another hath fulfilled the law**."

- Romans 13:10, "Love worketh no ill to his neighbor: therefore **love is the fulfilling of the law**."

No, we cannot fulfill the law. But He can. That is why He came—to fulfill what we needed to be fulfilled for us, because we could not do it in our own power. But to fulfill the law, we must love our neighbor as much as we love ourselves. That requires me to yield to the love in me—the love of my Master Teacher. It is His full purpose for me— to be a vessel that expresses His love.

To fulfill the law, we must love. If it is Christ who is fulfilling the law, then it must be His love that is being expressed. When we yield to His indwelling Holy Spirit, we are staying within the boundaries of more than just the law, or a set of rules; we are staying within the boundaries of Christ.

When our liberty from fulfilling the law ourselves is abused, we engage in self satisfaction. I can just tell you it won't be long before your ship is sunk. Galatians 5:13 refutes this behavior. Paul tells us that liberty from personally fulfilling the law will not get us out from under our obligation to love one another. "For, brethren, ye have been called unto liberty; only **use not liberty for an occasion to the flesh**, but **by love serve one another**."

Our ability to conform to the Old Testament law is predicated on one word—love! And that Old Testament law can only be fulfilled as we express Christ's love. We share our apprenticeship with others by fulfilling the law.

3. *We are only identified as disciples when we are expressing Christ's love.*

John 13:35 says, "By this shall all men know that ye are my disciples, if ye have **love** one to another." Is this generally how Christians interact with one another? No, not usually! According to Jesus, by what can a disciple be identified? If we hate one another? No, of course not! We are known as one of His disciples by how much we love one another. This is where all of our interpersonal victories and defeats are found—in *His* love that is *in* us.

Our hateful or selfish dispositions do not identify us as His disciples. We are only identified as disciples of Christ when we are expressing Christ's love. We share our apprenticeship with others by loving one another.

4. *In the last days, we must be careful to continue to express Christ's love.*

Matthew 24 brings to light an interesting truth about the days before Christ's return. It sadly depicts the Christian apathy that we see today.

"And as he sat upon the mount of Olives, the disciples came unto him privately, saying, Tell us, when shall these things be? and what *shall be* the sign of thy coming, and of the end of the world? And Jesus answered and said unto them, Take heed that no man deceive you. For many shall come in my name, saying, I am Christ; and shall deceive many. . .Then shall they deliver you up to be afflicted, and shall kill you: and ye shall be hated of all nations for my name's sake." – Matthew 24:3-5, 9

Jesus then describes how many Christians will respond to this unkind, abusive treatment:

"And then **shall many be offended**, and shall **betray one another**, and shall **hate one another**. And many false prophets shall rise, and shall deceive many. And because iniquity (self-righteous Christianity) shall abound, the love of many shall wax cold." – Matthew 24:10-12

I believe that the Bible teaches us that iniquity is when a believer tries to do good, but he does it in his own power. It is doing right things the wrong way or wrong things the right way. Not sinful, just not right. It is wrong. *Wrong* means "not suitable." All sin is wrong, but not all wrong is sin. Otherwise, I would sin when I turn my car in the wrong direction.

In the last days, Christians will be rejected because of their faith. Many Christians will wrongly respond by growing cold-hearted and loving less or improperly. If that is not clear evidence of what is experienced by many Christians today, then I don't know what is! Our self love is evident in almost every Christian arena.

This ought not be! As we are surely enduring what appear to be the last days, we must be careful to continue to express Christ's love when things wax worse and worse. We share our apprenticeship with others by expressing His love when we are being afflicted.

5. *Jesus makes Himself known to those who express Christ's love.*

"At that day ye shall know that I *am* in my Father, and **ye in me, and I in you**. He that hath my commandments, and keepeth them, he it is that loveth me: and he that loveth me shall be loved of my Father, and **I will love him, and will manifest myself to him**." – John 14:19-20

Oh my! Jesus said He will manifest Himself to those that abide in His love. You will know that He is in you and you are in Him! Glory to God, the greatest of these is love! You cannot be in Christ without yielding to and expressing His love. You cannot yield to or express His love unless you are abiding in Christ. They are synonymous. Yes, indeed they are identical positions. Are you in love with the One whose love is in you?!

Jesus was asked by one of his disciples, "…Lord, how is it that **thou wilt manifest thyself unto us**, and not unto the world? Jesus answered and said unto him, If a man **love** me, he will keep my words: and my Father will love him, and **we will come unto him, and make our abode with him**" (John 14:22-23). Yielding to His love *is* abiding with Christ.

If we would only fall in love with Him, then we will again fall in love with others. Yes, Jesus will make Himself known to those who express His love. This is how we can share our apprenticeship with others.

May I also point out that Jesus prayed for us that we might express Christ's love.

"O righteous Father, the world hath not known thee: but **I have known thee**, and these have known that thou hast sent me. And I have declared unto them thy name, and will declare *it*: **that the love wherewith thou hast loved me may be in them, and I in them.**" – John 17:25-26

C'mon naysayer. Stop your denials. If Jesus is not teaching us to end our harmful, hurtful, hateful, interpersonal selfishness that He may rule in our hearts, then what is He teaching us here?!

6. *The gift of the Holy Spirit allows us to express Christ's love.*

Peter told Jesus that he loved Him so much that he would die for Him. But Jesus knew that Peter's love was selfish. And just as Jesus foretold, Peter's selfish love was displayed when he denied Jesus three times! Yet upon Jesus' resurrection and ascension back to heaven, He gave this same Peter the gift of the Holy Spirit. Now Simon Peter could yield to God's love that lived within Him!

This is an amazing example of the difference between our ability to love versus submitting to our apprenticeship to allow His love to flow from us to those whom our Master Teacher has chosen. Peter's love denied Christ when put under pressure. But prior to Jesus' return to heaven, He knew that He would be leaving behind His Spirit to indwell His followers. They would now be able to yield to Him as successful graduates of His apprenticeship program! Realizing this, Jesus asked Peter to unconditionally love those whom Christ died to save.

"Simon (Peter), *son* of Jona, lovest thou me? Peter was grieved because he said unto him the third time, Lovest thou me? And he said unto him, Lord, thou knowest all things; thou knowest that I love thee. Jesus saith unto him, Feed my sheep." – John 21:17

What a thankless job that would be—feeding someone else's sheep? But that was how Jesus indicated that Peter could show that he truly loved Jesus. To be so unselfish, it would take Jesus' love that is garnered by yielding to the indwelling Holy Spirit.

It is only through the empowering gift and presence of the Holy Spirit that we can express Christ's love. Exposing the fruit of the Spirit in love is how we can share our apprenticeship with other potential apprentice.

7. *Each fruit of the Spirit is enjoyed as a result of expressing Christ's love.*

The nine fruits of the Spirit are listed in Galatians 5:22-23. These are the nine behaviors that are the outcome or result of the Holy Spirit living through us. The very first one listed is love! You may consider this improvable, but I believe, based on the vast

Scripture we have discussed, that yielding to love as we develop through our Savior's apprenticeship program creates a domino affect on the other eight fruits of the Spirit. When we yield to the fruit of the Spirit love, we will experience joy. Our joy then produces peace. This will calm us into being longsuffering, gentle, and good. Our faith will develop, rendering us meek amongst others and giving us the power to be temperate in all things.

As a matter of fact, the passage on the fruits of the Spirit is concluded with the following statement: "against such there is no law." Do you know what that means? It simply means that if we would love in His love and express the subsequent fruits that follow, we would not need a bunch of rules upon us. We would *remain* in Him and could *refrain* from being in sin.

With that said, the fruits of the Spirit are sure to be enjoyed if we would be obedient by expressing Christ's love. It is how we can share our apprenticeship with others ships in the sea.

8. *Living right is found in our expressing Christ's love.*

" According as he hath chosen us in him before the foundation of the world, that we should **be holy** and **without blame** before him in love." – Ephesians 1:4

To fulfill our call to be holy and blameless before Him we must be surrounded by the limits of (definition of "in") His love. Whose love would you think could keep us blameless and holy? It is not mine, that's for sure. It must be His! Surely, it is His love. We were chosen by God to live right in Him. In order to live right in Him, we must remain in His love. This expression of His love will cause us to live right. If we live right, we will share our apprenticeship with other weary sailors who set sail so often in their own power only to lose their course. Unable to find the energy to continue to live right in their own power, they stop working so hard and start drifting carelessly from the lake of lethargy into the sea of sin. They will soon find themselves adrift in the ocean of oppression.

9. *We are made complete in our expression of Christ's love.*

"But whoso **keepeth his word, in him** verily is the **love of God perfected**: hereby **know we that we are in him**." – I John 2:5

To be *perfected* means "completed or finished." Though our apprenticeship will never be complete this side of glory, our ability to set sail and teach others to do so likewise increases greatly when we add to our ship this weapon for war—love. This passage teaches us that one who expresses God's love is one who is obedient. Obedience to God comes from a life that expresses God's love. When God's love is perfected in us, we can be sure we are in Him. Expressing God's love will complete us. This is yet another way we can share our apprenticeship with others.

10. *God has something against us when we fail to express Christ's love.*

"Nevertheless I have somewhat against thee, because thou hast left thy first love. Remember therefore from whence thou art fallen, and repent, and do the first works; or else I will come unto thee quickly, and will remove thy candlestick out of his place, except thou repent." – Revelation 2:4-6

This was written to the church of Ephesus. According to the prior verses, this church looked as if they had it all together on the outside. However, deeper investigation into the heart of the body of believers proved to disconnect from His love—a failed apprenticeship.

I do not know for sure what they had done to prove that they had left their first love, but upon looking at the book of Ephesians, you can conclude that they had interpersonal problems within the church. Its teachings evidence that there were children disobeying parents, wives resisting the leadership of their husbands, fathers provoking their children to wrath, employees being insincere with employers, employers taking advantage of employees, citizens rebelling against God-ordained governmental leaders, people going to bed still angry with one another, stealing, laziness, bitterness, anger, resentment, and malice. Sounds to me like their "love for the brethren" had been forsaken.

Without love there is no candlestick. Without a candlestick, there is no candle. Without a candle there is no light. Without a light everyone remains in darkness. Why? As a result of leaving our love behind, others will be left behind someday, as well. We will often find that we ourselves will need to go back to our first love by simply repenting of our self love and submitting to the love that lies within us.

In closing, in John 15, Jesus went even deeper with His explanation of remaining as His apprentice by yielding to and expressing His love. Yes, we are learning that we need to love a lot more than we do. But it is not *more* love, it is *merely* love. For if it is our love, it is going to take much more than we have to give. But since it is merely His love, it is as simple as yielding to His internal promptings in our life.

"If ye keep my commandments, ye shall abide in my love ; even as I have kept my Father's commandments, and abide **in his love**. These things have I spoken unto you, that **my joy might remain in you, and** *that* **your joy might be full."** – John 15:10, 11

Could this verse be proving my earlier statements concerning the domino affect of love on the other fruits of the Spirit? Yes, indeed, we see that joy, the second fruit of the Spirit listed after love, is predicated on our first responding and remaining in His love.

"This is my commandment, That ye love one another, as I have loved you." – John 15:12

This commandment for our apprenticeship is to love as He has loved. It will lead us to abide in His love. So, we see that if we keep His commands (verse 10), we will abide in His love (or remain His apprentices). His single commandment that overrules all others is that we express love one to another as He has expressed His love toward us.

So that begs the question, how has He loved us that we might love one another the same way? And who are these friends to whom and for whom God expresses such great love?

The answers are in the next verses:

"Greater love hath no man than this, that a man lay down his life for his friends. Ye are my friends, if ye do whatsoever I command you." – John 15:13,14

Then finally, in verse 16, Jesus turns His attention back to the fruit that He expects us to bear as a result of our deep, abiding relationship that remains in Him:

"Ye have not chosen me, but I have chosen you, and ordained you, **that ye should go and bring forth fruit**, and *that* **your fruit should remain**: that whatsoever ye shall ask of the Father in my name, he may give it you." – John 15:16

To gain our position in Christ, we must be saved. To retain that position, we must live a life yielded to His apprenticeship program, as led by the Holy Ghost.

When we fail to live the Spirit-led life that IS Christ, then we step out from our position of abiding in Christ and remain in the dangerous position of self control. We can do good, but it will be in our own power. Eventually, we will probably give in and actually do something bad because we are too weak to control ourselves long term. This is where God's conviction or chastening will be His symbolic gesture of love.

But this does not have to be the case. You can

regain our role in His apprenticeship program. In doing so, we might experience afresh and anew the presence of the Spirit. But what does it take? It takes the same process that it took for God to regain access to your spirit. As we discussed in our topical books on addictions, there needs to be a crucifixion, a time of burial, and a subsequent resurrection in the power of His might! Then you are back in His program for apprenticeship; but only as long as we will submit to His leading and His love.

In conclusion, we cannot love *others* with His love until we truly love *Him* with His love. If we love Him, we will serve others—unselfishly. Jude 21-22 admonishes us, "Keep yourselves **in, the love of God**, looking for the mercy of our Lord Jesus Christ unto eternal life. And of some have compassion, making a difference."

First Corinthians 13:13 states, "And now abideth faith, hope, charity, these three; but the greatest of these is charity (or, love)." God's greatest gift is love, and it is through this portal of love that all other gifts are given. Our greatest gift to God and man should be our transparent cooperation with Him in yielding to His prompting to love Him and others. If you love Him, you will serve Him. If you serve Him, you will love Him.

Below are some characteristics taken out of our student textbook <u>Nevertheless I Live</u>. Let's see how your apprenticeship program is going. Let's look at the characteristics of love described in First Corinthians 13. Charity is an outward manifestation of our love, either ours or His. If it is our love, it will expect something in return or reject continued expression if something is not given in return. If it is His love, then it will resemble the following list:

My charity, or love for others, should:

suffereth long, and is kind
   —*puts up with inconveniences*

envieth not
   —*lifts up others; not self*

vaunteth not itself
   —*is not stuck up*

doth not behave unseemly
   —*acts right*

seeketh not her own
 —*looks for what is right*

is not easily provoked
 —*responds right*

thinketh no evil
 —*thinks right*

rejoiceth not in iniquity
 —*doesn't get excited about what's not right*

rejoiceth in truth
 —*gets excited about what is right*

beareth all things
 —*carries the weight*

believeth all things
 —*gives the benefit of the doubt*

hopeth all things
 —*hopes for the best*

endureth all things
 —*keeps on keeping on*

never fails
 —*works every time!*

How do you serve God? Remember, it is a manifestation of your love. The above list helps us to gauge the apprenticeship of our battleship. Are you sea worthy?

CONCLUSION:
A BATTLESHIP NAMED PARTNERSHIP

"Now he that planteth and he that watereth are one: and every man shall receive his own reward according to his own labour. For we are labourers together with God: ye are God's husbandry, ye are God's building. According to the grace of God which is given unto me, as a wise masterbuilder, I have laid the foundation, and another buildeth thereon. But let every man take heed how he buildeth thereupon."
– I Corinthians 3:8-10

D id you grow up with the stories of the Lone Ranger? This masked lawman "led the fight for law and order in the early days of the West." He traveled across the prairie bringing justice to the American frontier. I heard somewhere that the definition of a true intellectual is a person who listens to the *William Tell Overture* without thinking of the Lone Ranger! But there's something you need to remember about the Lone Ranger. He may have been the last of the Rangers, but he was never alone!

Everywhere the Lone Ranger rode; his faithful Indian companion Tonto was by his side. God did not call and commission us as battleships to sail and fight alone. To be the Christian God has called you to be, you need His people. As the Apostle Paul said, "we are labourers together." We are on the same team.

Notice also that we are not just working together in partnership with each other; we are working together in partnership with *God*. When I think of this truth, I think of David's good friend Jonathan. As the son of King Saul, the people of Israel looked to him as a leader. When the Philistines came against the Israelites in battle, Jonathan and his armor bearer went out to fight against them alone. God gave them a great victory, which led to the deliverance of the chosen people.

At the end of the battle, the people said this about Jonathan, "He hath wrought (worked) with

God this day" (I Sam. 14:45). Why did Jonathan face the foe and win the victory? Faith. First Samuel 14:6-7 says, "And Jonathan said to the young man that bare his armour, Come, and let us go over unto the garrison these uncircumcised: it may be that the Lord will work for us: for there is no restraint to the Lord to save by many or by few. And his armourbearer said unto him, Do all that is in thine heart: turn thee; behold, I am with thee according to thy heart." (Notice a partnership has begun!)

There are many things that people can say about us and the ship in which we sail into battle each and every day. But I believe that nothing could be better said than that we have been working in partnership with others and with Almighty God to fight His enemy and win the victory. But remember that it is not our strength, but our availability coupled with faith that makes us partners in the work of His kingdom.

So how's your ship shaped today? Are you, like the *HMS Hood,* sailing into battle unprepared and with your armor in disarray? Or are you like Jonathan, stepping out in faith, fully trusting God to give you the victory? If these eight "ships" are in order in your life, you're ready to face the enemy as God's battleship.

And let me give you one final word of encouragement. All of us fail sometimes. All of us fall short. We lose battles. But defeat doesn't have to be final.

On December 7, 1941, the Japanese launched their surprise attack on Pearl Harbor. Eight American battleships were lying at anchor that Sunday morning when the attack started. Though all eight suffered varying degrees of damage, only two, the *Arizona* and the *Oklahoma* were destroyed. The other six were repaired, and put back into service. The *Nevada* was sent to fight in Europe, where she took part in the D-Day invasion of Normandy. The *Tennessee, Pennsylvania, Maryland, California* and *West Virginia* all fought the Japanese, including taking part in the last surface naval battle during the invasion of the Philippines.

You may have been hit by the enemy's bombs. Your life may have been damaged. Other people may look at you and think there is nothing you can do and that your life is hopeless. But God can make you new. God can use you again in His service and for His glory. Get back in the fight today! Be the Battleship—Partnership! Partner with Him and even with others to save other sailors and build better ships. Join Him and win with a partnership in worship. You will talk *with* God. Join Him and win with a partnership in discipleship, and you will get to know *about* God. Join Him and win with a partnership in relationship, and you will get to *know* Him. Join Him and win with a partnership in fellowship, and you will get to *enjoy* Him. Join Him and win with a partnership in followship, and you will *find* Him, lest you lose you way. Join Him and win with a partnership in leadership, and you will get *to* Him, bringing others along the way. Join Him and win with a partnership in stewardship, and you will get to give willingly *of* Him. Join Him and win with a partnership in apprenticeship, and you will develop an urge to serve. Join Him in a partnership as a battleship, and the victories will be won with regularity.

"But thanks be to God, which giveth us the victory through our Lord Jesus Christ."
  – I Corinthians 15:57

Steve Curington
President and Founder of
Reformers Unanimous International

Steven Curington is the husband of Lori and the father of their five children: Charity, Chase, Channing, Chance, and Cherish. He is the founder of Reformers Unanimous International, a faith based, local-church discipleship program that ministers to the addicted - both within and without the body of Christ. Mr. Curington travels extensively, presenting the ministry and starting chapters of this fast growing support group and discipleship classes in Bible-preaching churches all over the world. He also holds Regional Training Conferences for churches to meet the needs of the addicted in their communities. He is a popular conference speaker and the host of the new radio broadcast Found and Unbound. More information on Steven Curington's ministries, including Reformers Unanimous, is available at his web site: www.reformu.com. Reformers Unanimous International is headquarted in the historical downtown district of Rockford, Illinois.

Reformers Unanimous Material

"It's Personal" Daily Journal
Classic Size

RU looking for a devotional tool that's more than a glorified notebook? Discover the revolutionary tool that has helped many individuals walk and talk with Christ and have a victorious Christian life. The 90-day *"It's Personal"* Daily Journal is a proven method for developing a dynamic love-relationship with Jesus Christ. This journal is our #1 selling product in America! It comes complete with an instructional CD explaining how to use the journal and its five forms of communication in order to maximize your personal walk with God.

(7x 8.5 size, 90 -day supply,
Includes instructional CD)

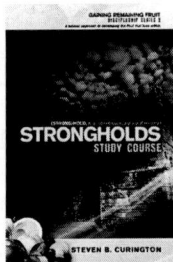

#CE-111 **$15.00**

Strongholds Study Course
Gaining Remaining Fruit Discipleship Series **I**

This book represents your first book, the Strongholds Study Course. It is followed by the Uphold and Behold Study Courses. These three workbooks represent the entire GRF Discipleship Course. It is available, as shown here for adults, and has also been developed for teens and young children as well. No matter your age or struggle, the GRF Discipleship Series can help you know God in a more personal and intimate manner.

#CE-103 **$15.00**

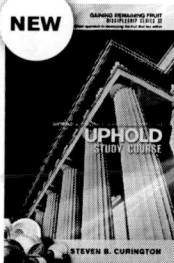

NEW

Uphold Study Course
Gaining Remaining Fruit Discipleship Series **II**

This book represents your second book, the Upholds Study Course. It is preceded by the Strongholds and followed by the Behold Study Courses. These three workbooks represent the entire GRF Discipleship Course. It is available, as shown here for adults, and it has been developed for teens and young children as well. No matter your age or struggle, the GRF Discipleship Series can help you know God in a more personal and intimate manner.

#CE-203 **$20.00**

COMING SOON!

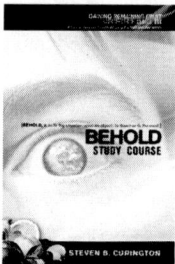

Behold Study Course
Gaining Remaining Fruit Discipleship Series **III**

This book represents your third book, the Behold Study Course. It is preceded by the Strongholds and Uphold Study Courses. These three workbooks represent the entire GRF Discipleship Course. It is available, as shown here for adults, and it has been developed for teens and young children as well. No matter your age or struggle, the GRF Discipleship Series can help you know God in a more personal and intimate manner.

#CE-303 **$20.00**

GRF I, II, III
Gaining Remaining Fruit Discipleship Series
Complete Set

#CE-403 **$49.00**

reformu.com or 815-986-0460